'The book is more than a chronicle of the instit
analysis of the institute as a community from the
apy theory. It contains first person experiences
and blood of the institute. It is difficult not to be ......
some of the drama. It is a chronicle that includes strong personalities, rivai-
ries, generational clashes, bruises, loyalty, love, and friendships.'

Dan Bloom, *from the Foreword*

'As a Gestalt therapist trained in the West Coast tradition, the importance
of this book lies for me in the demystification of the New York Institute, the
starting place of our approach. It documents honestly the power-oriented
style of communication and the "tradition of aggression" as part of Gestalt
therapy from the beginning and allows us to follow the process of democratization in which women played an important role. The book is an important contribution to understanding where we all come from and who we are.'

Bernd Bocian, *Author of* Fritz Perls in Berlin 1893–
1933: Expressionism, Psychoanalysis, Judaism

'Václav Mikolášek has done an impressive job of showing how historical
changes over several decades within the New York Institute for Gestalt therapy, first established by gestalt therapy's founders, reflect the evolution of
the theory and practice of gestalt therapy itself. He traces the Institute's
shifts from autocratic rule to democratic consensus, from patriarchy to diversity, from individualistic ego-based aggression to an inclusive relational
atmosphere, and onward to the current expansion of the relational into field
theory. Mikolášek's book is an important and illuminating contribution to
the history of psychotherapy.'

Michael Vincent Miller, *PhD, Current President, New
York Institute for Gestalt Therapy, Author,* Intimate
Terrorism *and* Teaching a Paranoid to Flirt

The History, Theory and Community of Gestalt Therapy

Exploring the New York Institute

This book tells the story of the community at the New York Institute for Gestalt Therapy (NYIGT) as it evolved in connection with the highly regarded theory it produced, examining some important turning points for the institute spanning the period from the early 1970s until 2020 and describing the more large-scale changes the community underwent.

Through chronologically ordered chapters, the history of the NYIGT is written in a documentary-style narrative complete with the voices of contemporary witnesses embedded into the storyline. The book explores the aggressiveness during community meetings that the institute was once known for, how the LGBTQIA community shaped the institute from the beginning, what changed when the institute began to be run democratically, its feminist revolution, as well as recent developments and the institute's current group processes.

This historically rich work is essential reading for Gestalt therapists, other professionals interested in Gestalt approaches, and readers interested in the history of Gestalt therapy.

Václav Mikolášek was born in 1983 in Prague. He graduated in computer science before moving to Vienna where he studied psychotherapy at the Sigmund Freud University. He lives in Vienna and works as a psychotherapist.

The Gestalt Therapy Book Series

The Istituto di Gestalt series of Gestalt therapy books emerges from the ground of a growing interest in theory, research and clinical practice in the Gestalt community. The members of the Scientific and Editorial Boards have been committed for many years to the process of supporting research and publications in our field: through this series we want to offer our colleagues internationally the richness of the current trends in Gestalt therapy theory and practice, underpinned by research. The goal of this series is to develop the original principles in hermeneutic terms: to articulate a relational perspective, namely a phenomenological, aesthetic, field-oriented approach to psychotherapy. It is also intended to help professions and to support a solid development and dialogue of Gestalt therapy with other psychotherapeutic methods.

The series includes original books specifically created for it, as well as translations of volumes originally published in other languages. We hope that our editorial effort will support the growth of the Gestalt therapy community; a dialogue with other modalities and disciplines; and new developments in research, clinics and other fields where Gestalt therapy theory can be applied (e.g., organizations, education, political and social critique and movements).

We would like to dedicate this Gestalt Therapy Book Series to all our mentors and colleagues who have sown fruitful seeds in our minds and hearts.

For a full list of titles in this series, please visit www.routledge.com/Gestalt-Therapy/book-series/GESTHE and www.gestaltitaly.com

The History, Theory and Community of Gestalt Therapy

Exploring the New York Institute

Václav Mikolášek

Routledge
Taylor & Francis Group

LONDON AND NEW YORK

Designed cover image: © Zara Pfeifer

First published 2023
by Routledge
4 Park Square, Milton Park, Abingdon, Oxon OX14 4RN

and by Routledge
605 Third Avenue, New York, NY 10158

Routledge is an imprint of the Taylor & Francis Group, an informa business

© 2023 Václav Mikolášek

British Library Cataloguing-in-Publication Data
A catalogue record for this book is available from the British Library

Library of Congress Cataloging-in-Publication Data
Names: Mikolášek, Václav, author.
Title: The history, theory and community of gestalt therapy :
exploring the New York institute / Václav Mikolášek.
Description: New York, NY : Routledge, 2023. |
Series: Gestalt therapy book series |
Includes bibliographical references and index. |
Identifiers: LCCN 2022032302 | ISBN 9781032283722 (hbk) |
ISBN 9781032283739 (pbk) | ISBN 9781003296539 (ebk)
Subjects: LCSH: Gestalt psychology.
Classification: LCC BF203 .M57 2023 | DDC 150.19/82—dc23/eng/20220921
LC record available at https://lccn.loc.gov/2022032302

ISBN: 978-1-032-28372-2 (hbk)
ISBN: 978-1-032-28373-9 (pbk)
ISBN: 978-1-003-29653-9 (ebk)

DOI: 10.4324/9781003296539

Typeset in Times New Roman
by codeMantra

Contents

Acknowledgment

It is a pleasure to have the opportunity here to express my gratitude to those who helped this book along. First of all I want to thank my interviewees who shared their stories with generosity and openness: thank you Adam, Burt, Dan, Gayla, Elinor, Erv, Lee, Margherita, Peter, Perry, Ruella, and Susan for your support, kindness, lunches, and everything! I am indebted to my editor Margherita Spagnuolo Lobb for making the initial idea of a book a concrete possibility, to Bernd Bocian and Michael Vincent Miller for their endorsements, to Stefania Benini and Katie Randall for their work on the production, and to the peer reviewers who shall remain anonymous. I also want to thank Martin Jandl and Brigitte Rasmus whose enthusiasm and support was very important for me. Three special thanks are reserved for: Dan Bloom for the clever and fun foreword which in its form and content reflects the modus operandi of the NYIGT, Adam Weitz for his kind and gentle afterword, and Burt Lazarin for the accommodation! I am grateful to Molly Rawle from The Gestalt Journal Press, Inc. for permission to quote so copiously from Perls, Hefferline, and Goodman's *Gestalt Therapy: Excitement and Growth in the Human Personality*. This is not an exhaustive list of all the help I have received and the friendships made along. I regret the omissions but they are safe in my heart's memory.

Foreword

Just What Has This to Do with the New York Institute for Gestalt Therapy?[1]

By Dan Bloom

"If you think you know who we are, think again."

I used that phrase to invite people to take another look at the institute when I was president of the New York Institute for Gestalt Therapy (hereinafter, NYIGT) for two terms, from 2001 to 2005. We all knew that there were impressions of us formed over the years that had congealed into various fixed gestalten that variously attracted and repelled people. Decades of grinding out gestalt therapy and grinding people over the millstone of change inevitably left its marks. We generated heat, light, smoke, and fire. Fame and infamy. Impressions—and misimpressions.

We celebrated our fiftieth anniversary during my term. Our 50th anniversary conference "gestalt Alive! Fifty Years, Developing, Living, Gestalt Therapy" June 12–15, 2003, would showcase our refreshed gestalt as a community committed to the creativity of contacting.

I had no illusions. Fixed gestalten are stubborn. We psychotherapists know this well.

And this brings me to the book at hand. This introduction is prefatory. It will not precapitulate or summarize the book to come. Among the introduction's purposes is to suggest that "If you think you know who we are, think again" and to consider what brings you to take a look at us at all. And if this is your first look at us or if you come to this book unfamiliar with the world of gestalt therapy, then consider this introduction as an idiosyncratic welcome.

The NYIGT was sustained for decades by an active membership that expanded and compressed as times changed; yet the institute never, ever, hesitated, faltered, missed a breath or a step in more than 70 years of uninterrupted, continuous functioning despite chronic crises. It organized four conferences, two of which attracted more than 100 international registrants. Its members have been training therapists just about everywhere in the world and have been publishing in just about every gestalt therapy journal and in many edited books, if they have not written and are writing their own.

The institute is a subject of interest for many gestalt therapists throughout the gestalt world. Yet it is important not to assume to know why. Is it merely because of its history? Its influence? That it cleaves to a particular tradition or pure model of gestalt therapy? I reject the fallacy of NYIGT exceptionalism, which believes we are special—a one of a kind fount of gestalt wisdom, truth, or purity.

I invite the reader to use the experience of reading this book as an opportunity to explore these questions. The book that follows is more than a chronicle of the institute's history. It is a critical analysis of the institute as a community from the perspective of gestalt therapy theory. It is comprehensive and at the same time provides a gestalt-socio-historical-analysis of the institute that uncovers important developments in the social history of gestalt therapy theory. Even further, it more broadly maps the world situation within which the institute functioned.

The book is also the story of gestalt therapy itself through the lives of its founders and those who inherited the institute, the house they built, as well as those who carry on its structure, maintain it, build additions, and even renovate it and in so doing, take seriously gestalt therapy theory and practice.

The book contains first person experiences that give a sense of the flesh and blood of the institute. It is difficult not to be stimulated—provoked—by some of the drama. It is a chronicle that includes strong personalities, rivalries, generational clashes, bruises, loyalty, love, and friendships. Points of view are embedded in personal situations crisscrossed with histories scribbled in flesh and blood. Forty-year-old grievances might seem still fresh. And current bonds of community will appear vivid. Some of the anecdotes are humorous and some might be disturbing. The narrative has enough breadth and complexity to support a variety of fixed gestalts or impressions about the NYIGT. At the same time, it contains enough analysis that could prevent these descriptions from congealing into fixities and even to change some previously held points of view. So, "if you think you know who we are" consider this book, and "think again."

This introduction proposes a gestalt-phenomenological approach to reading this book, which invites you, the reader, to bring yourself into the process itself as much as possible. I will explain.

There are many different ways people characterize the institute. Some of them are simple observations of the institute based on perceptions at particular times and places as a function of the atmospheric changes of the institute or of the incremental modifications of gestalt therapy itself. After all, the 70-year history of gestalt therapy has seen us move from a more or less individualist original perspective through the relational, dialogical, and field-emergent orientations. Not all of these become fixed gestalten as peoples' characterizations change. But some characterizations have been persistent and remain statements not only of who we were and have been, but of who we are and will always be. These would be fixed gestalten of the institute that I have been referring to. It is useful to discover the structure of these fixities as well as the ground that supports them prior to reading this book. These fixities are potentially background shadows that affect how readers approach the coming text. That is, they constitute preconceptions or foreknowledge. Even the very basis of anyone's interest in the NYIGT itself might be considered. Why care about the institute at all? A person's ground might already contain some history with the institute, either through direct first-hand, full-blooded experiences or from information communicated across the infinitely extended networks of hearsay narratives, written, or spoken. No one comes to this book's discussion of the institute as a blank slate to be inscribed upon. Fore-contacting begins already sedimented with unnoticed history.

Consequently, the reader must be willing to having preconceptions challenged, disturbed, confirmed, or destructured by reading this text. To read this book, then, is to allow yourself to be as if read by this book. Then it would be fair to wonder, "just what has this book to do with the NYIGT"—your preconception of the NYIGT.

How, then, are these preconceptions brought into the light? Phenomenologists say the obvious is often what we most often overlook.

The grip of the hermeneutic circle is unbreakable: we understand from within our understanding. We gestalt therapists refer to this as the contextual method of argument, taking warrant from *Gestalt Therapy, Excitement and Growth in the Human Personality* (Perls, Hefferline, and Goodman 1994). In any person's condition of experience, his or her opinion is the opinion that must behold. That is, any particular idea is only understandable with reference to its total context including the "social milieu and the personal 'defenses' of the observer" (Perls, Hefferline, and Goodman 1994, 20). This gestalt-phenomenological approach puts this differently.

Understanding and meaning-making are functions of contacting, which is emergent of a ground that is inclusive of the reader and what is read. Each of you will be reading this book in the context of who you are, your own experiences with gestalt therapy, your professional lives, and your sense of yourself in your own gestalt therapy community. Or, if you are unfamiliar with this world, you are coming to this book with preconceptions based on different impressions.[2] In your reading of the book, the NYIGT becomes a living figure against and in relation to a changing ground that includes you. The figure/ground of the NYIGT already includes each of us since no gestalt floats out there as if disconnected from the ground. To some extent, smaller or greater, we approach this book and the institute from a personal and social ground in which it already has acquired meanings.

These are taken for granted, unnoticed, presuppositions about the institute that are specific to you and to your particular gestalt world or community. For example, the view of NYIGT is different from the gestalt community in Chile, from the gestalt community in Toronto, from one institute in Manhattan to another, or one institute in Russia to another. We are

important here and there, unimportant there and here, inspiring there, discouraging here.[3] The NYIGT has a different function in each gestalt world.
Consider, then, if the institute carries any significance—or reputation—
in your particular community, institute, among your peers, colleagues,
socio-professional world, and so on. Now reflect on what you already know
about the institute. What do you know, what have you heard, what have
you already experienced? Are these firsthand experiences in meetings, with
members, at conferences, or what you heard or read? Some of you might
have had an exciting experience at an institute function. Others of you might
have come away from a meeting with another impression altogether. These
could count now as preconceptions or background from which you will approach this book.

Now when you turn to the text itself, with your presuppositions in your
conscious awareness, notice the texture, qualities, tone, brightness, contour,
rhythm of your interest, and even the pace of your reading as you read.
This may mean that you will have to pause and step back to reflect from
time to time since contactful reading itself is an immersive experience. Yet
notice how you have been contacting the emerging figures. These are the
aesthetic qualities of contacting, which are indicators of the nature of your
engagement and interest. What are you discovering? What preconception is
confirmed? Have what you have taken for granted about the institute and
gestalt therapy somehow been challenged? You are allowing yourself to be
read by the book to the extent you are discovering things about yourself
and, perhaps, allowing new figures of the NYIGT to form.

This is gestalt-phenomenological approach to reading this book. Your
presuppositions identified, hopefully you are then open to the qualities
of contacting in your reading. Your reading, following the language of a
gestalt-phenomenology, is the intentionality of contacting. The qualities
of the emerging figure itself affirm a renewed figure of the institute, a new
"intentional object," or better, in our terms, a new figure/ground of the
intentionality of contacting.

I invite you, then, into an aggressively contactful reading of the book in
which you put into question your already formed assumptions about the
institute. I invite you to bring yourself into reading and turn it into an explicitly relational process. Engage with the institute and the people who leap
from the narrative. Let the book push back at you as you engage with it.

Although this is addressed later in the book, it is impossible for me to
conclude this introduction without acknowledging that we are in a world
shuddering through the pandemic of COVID-19, the catastrophes of climate
change, and the tragedies of racial violence.

All of us have been thrown by the pandemic into the necessity of techno-
phenomenological contacting. Contacting in a techno-phenomenological
field pushes us to the frontiers of our understandings of gestalt therapy and,
perhaps, of the institute itself. For decades the institute had been grappling

with this in terms of ways to integrate non-local members into meetings. But now we are forced to no longer hold in-person meetings. Every institute meeting now demands us to assume a presence at an unfamiliar contact-boundary. This asks us for a new commitment to explore potentialities of the contact-boundary as the phenomenal location of contacting and contacting as creative adjusting to the possibilities and impossibilities of the situation.

Or perhaps this is nothing at all new about this for a protean institute that, while having a formal structure, shape-shifted freely in response to the calls from within and without, to the pleas and needs of its members, and to the urgencies of the world in which it existed—and exists.

If you think you know who we are, maybe this book is a way for you to look at us again.

We at the institute are always looking at ourselves—again and again and again. Perhaps you will discover this as a theme of the book that follows.

Notes

1 With tongue in cheek, I am paraphrasing a controversial question posed by Isadore From to a young gestalt therapist who just presented her work for the first time at a monthly meeting of the institute. Her presentation was on gestalt therapy and mandalas. "Just what does this have to do with gestalt therapy?" asked Isadore. That sentence has become emblematic for the carnivorous culture of the NYIGT in the 1980s. I believe he began the sentence with the now unacceptable, "My dear..." Those days he would have used the same words for a man or a woman.
2 In 2004, I introduced myself as president of the NYIGT to Eugene Gendlin. "Oh, so you people are still around. Are you still making such a racket?"
3 And, of course, we are mostly unknown in many, many places.

Bibliography

Perls, F., Hefferline, R., & Goodman, P. (1951). *Gestalt therapy: Excitement and growth in human personality*. Gestalt Journal Press.

Introduction

My goal for this book is to tell a story of the community at the New York Institute for Gestalt Therapy (NYIGT) as it evolved in connection with the theory it produced. There are many stories about this avant-garde institute and they are so well known that every gestalt therapist is on a first-name basis with Laura, Fritz, and Paul. What is less known is how the institute and its community evolved when the founders either left or withdrew and the younger generation of members took over. I want to resume where the other stories left off and continue the narrative. I look at some important moments of the institute spanning roughly the period from the early 1970s until 2020 and describe the changes that the community underwent.

I have attempted to provide a coherent narrative in a documentary style so that one can hear the voices of contemporary witnesses embedded in a storyline. The chapters are ordered chronologically as much as it was possible, but there are of course inevitable overlaps. At the same time, I wanted to provide a certain second level to the narrative in the form of theoretical discussions. This seemed to me especially important because the New York Institute is in itself a gestalt experiment, and in a kind of feedback loop the community develops in an ongoing dialogue with the theory it produces. In the words of Dan Bloom: "From the very beginning the community and the theory were identical because the community emerged out of the teaching of the theory. People gathered around learning and teaching and they lived the theory with one another" (Bloom, 2019).

The community of the New York Institute is a vividly living thing that defies all attempts at reification, and if this book manages to capture this liveliness, then I am happy with the result. I describe *some* important events and provide space for the voices of *some* of those who witnessed them. That means, unfortunately, that I omit other events and exclude other voices.

I regret, for example, that I was not able to secure an interview with Carl Hodges, without whom the story of the democratization of the institute has left a big blank space. Also the new generation of people, who will be the next to inherit the institute are not well represented in this book. And there are others whom I do not know and who would have important

DOI: 10.4324/9781003296539-1

stories to tell. My choice of the interview partners was based on my intuition and one interview led to another.

The Interviews

The majority of the interviews took place in 2019 during my stay in the United States. In 2021, in order to better cover the topic of the institute's increasing internationality, I have added two more interviews. One with Margherita Spagnuolo Lobb and the other with Peter Philippson. Eight interviews were done in person; seven in New York and one (with Erving Polster) in La Jolla, California. The rest took place online. The average duration of an interview was approximately one hour. The exception is the interview with Adam Weitz, the then serving President of the New York Institute, whom I interviewed in two online sessions and that resulted in a total duration of 130 minutes.

My goal for the interviews was to obtain personal accounts of the communal life at the institute. I was interested in first-hand stories and experiences that none other than the interviewed person could relate to. Because of the distinctly personal nature of the matter, I have decided against a structured interview with a set of fixed questions. I wanted to allow space for surprises and be able to follow up on the unexpected, if it raised my interest.

Typically, I started the interview with a general statement that I am interested in the communal life and the personal story and asked the interviewed person how she or he first came to the institute and what the first impressions were like. Afterward, I let myself be guided by whatever came. If I got the impression that my interview partner left the first-person perspective and started to relate to stories that are generally known, I would then try to steer the conversation again toward the personal account.

Overview

The following chapter deals with the topic of the aggressiveness of the community meetings that the institute was once notorious for. Even though the atmosphere has changed since the 1990s, the institute still grapples with the heritage of the founders who "hammered at each other" every week (Wysong & Rosenfeld, 1988, 79). Some of those I interviewed still carry scars from the times of combativeness and some miss the liveliness of the discussions. The theoretical part in this chapter focuses on the concepts of dental aggression, introjections, and organismic self-regulation. In order to understand the role of the theory in this respect, I make a short detour to the Cleveland Institute and describe the very different communal atmosphere that was to be found there.

The New York Institute was the first psychology organization in the United States that did not consider homosexuality a pathology, and from

its very beginning since the 1950s, it attracted people from the LGBT+ community. Only decades later did the institute's view become mainstream. In
Chapter 2, I explore how the LGBT+ community helped to shape the institute. I describe an organization called Identity House, which offers peer
counsel services to LGBT+ people and which was envisioned in the early
1970s by Patrick Kelley—a member of the institute—as an organization
based on gestalt principles. Even though there is not an explicit cooperation
between the institute and Identity House, there is a significant overlap in
terms of people and theory. In the theoretical part of this chapter, I explore
the role of Paul Goodman, look critically at the explicit conceptualization
of homosexuality in gestalt therapy theory, and identify the gestalt principle
of figure formation as the actual concept that was supportive to the LGBT+
community.

Toward the end of the 1980s, the institute arrived at a turning point: no
one from the Fellows wanted to serve another term as the Vice President,
Treasurer, or Secretary. They therefore turned to other members and asked
them to take up the administrative work. However, the younger generation
did not want to do the work without having any decision power and refused
to take part in what they saw as an autocratic governance of the Fellows.
The younger members had a different vision: they wanted the institute to
be a membership-run organization that is governed in a democratic fashion. They organized themselves and, in the course of two years, rewrote the
bylaws and revolutionized the institute. In Chapter 3, I look at these democratization changes and provide a discussion of the theory that supported
them; the then new focus on group dynamics in gestalt group therapy gets
special attention in this context. The changes at the institute happened in a
specific historical situation: at the end of the 1980s, there were democratization efforts going on in many different parts of the world. I conclude the
chapter with a hypothesis that thanks to gestalt therapy theory, the institute
is acutely sensitive to the phenomena of the wider field.

In Chapter 4, I describe the feminist revolution that took place at the institute in 1990. At the end of the 1980s, a group of women organized into a
caucus and questioned what they perceived to be a male-dominated culture
of the large monthly meetings. They were meeting regularly over a couple
years and explored alternative group processes where women would feel
comfortable. They combined feminist perspectives and gestalt therapy theory in their explorations and presented their findings to the membership in
the form of two gestalt experiments. These experiments had a profound and
lasting effect on the institute's culture, which then became more inclusive
and welcoming. This change also brought some detrimental developments
and I provide a discussion of what Dan Bloom identifies as a new fixed gestalt of the institute's group process: since the 1990s, the new focus on group
dynamics and the intensified exploration of the field conditions in which a
group operates seems to prevent sharp figures of one-on-one discussions

and conflicts between individuals. In the theoretical discussion, I argue that the feminist perspective in general and the efforts of the women's caucus in particular represent a direct challenge to gestalt therapy's individualistic heritage.

In Chapter 5, I describe the history of the increasing internationality of the institute. At the beginning of the 1990s, the first couple of gestalt therapists from Europe joined the institute and eventually became Full Members. Since then, the institute gradually opened itself to the international community. This opening happened in two directions: on one hand, the members of the institute were actively writing and publishing, gained in international recognition and started to be invited as trainers and traveled overseas; on the other hand, the institute welcomed new members from abroad. Especially in recent years and in connection with the COVID-19 pandemics, there was a rapid increase in the numbers of international members. Currently, the number of members who do not live in New York has been growing faster than the number of local members. This ongoing demographic change raises important questions about the future shape and function of the institute and the value of face-to-face meetings. Lee Zevy at one point suggested that the institute should have a non-local President. Although this suggestion did not take roots, it points to the fact that the institute is re-thinking its function and form.

Interviewed Persons

Dan Bloom

Dan Bloom was Vice President of the New York Institute in 1997–1999 and then President for two terms from 2001 to 2005. He practiced as a lawyer before becoming a psychotherapist and social worker. He was also a peer counselor at the Identity House. He joined the institute in 1976 and trained with Laura Perls, Isadore From, Richard Kitzler, and Patrick Kelley. Currently, he is a fellow of the institute, which is a distinction for members who are seen as carriers of the institute's tradition, history, and values. Bloom's theoretical interest lies in the foundational gestalt therapy theory within the contemporary relational perspective.

Elinor Greenberg

Elinor Greenberg trained in gestalt therapy in California with Robert Resnick before she moved to New York and joined the institute, where she trained with Isadore From. She joined the institute in 1972 and became a Full Member three years after that. She left the institute some years later and returned in 2008. Besides having been Vice President of the New York Institute between 2015 and 2017, she also served as a co-chair of the program committee that compiles the institute's educational program. She is a graduate of the Masterson Institute and specialized in the diagnosis and treatment of people with narcissistic, schizoid, and borderline personality disorders.

Susan Gregory

Susan Gregory joined the institute in 1990 and served as the President from 2007 to 2009. Before studying gestalt therapy, she was a professional opera singer. She studied Gindler's Arbeit am Menschen, a breath and bodywork therapeutic approach. Her practical and theoretical interest lies in the embodied aspects of gestalt therapy and she published on this subject extensively. Besides being a psychotherapist, she also teaches singing.

Gayla Feinstein

Gayla Feinstein is one of the initiators of the institute's women's caucus, which had a significant impact on the culture of the institute. Feinstein is a women's rights activist and integrates feminism into her therapeutic work. She started as a massage and art therapist and later became interested in gestalt therapy. Her first therapist and trainer was Karen Humphrey, a fellow and one of the early members of the institute. Karen Humphrey, Laura Perls, and Richard Kitzler were some of her mentors. Feinstein was President from 1997 to 1999 and served three times as Vice President.

Ruella Frank

Ruella Frank practices psychotherapy in New York City, where she is a director of the Center for Somatic Studies, training faculty at the Gestalt Associates for Psychotherapy, adjunct faculty at Gestalt Institute of Toronto, and a Full Member of the NYIGT. She was a student of Laura Perls and Richard Kitzler, among others. Laura Perls' integration of coordinated movements, the primary supports for contacting, was what drew Frank to gestalt therapy. She continues this movement-oriented tradition in her research and work.

Burt Lazarin

Burt Lazarin joined the institute in the 1980s via Identity House, where over the years, he held both the Executive and Clinical Director positions. He served as the institute's Secretary, Vice President, and then as the President from 2005 until 2007. He trained with Laura Perls, Bud Feder, Ruth Ronall, and Patrick Kelley. Karen Humphrey was his supervisor, and Richard Kitzler has been his therapist for many years.

Perry Klepner

Perry Klepner is a fellow and a past president of the New York Institute. He trained with Isadore From, Richard Kitzler, and Laura Perls. He has been on the faculty of several institutes and in his private practice provides training, supervision and individual, couples, and group therapy. Klepner's knowledgeability of the original theory and the history of the institute was an important source of information for this work. Additionally, Klepner leads reading groups, where the original text Gestalt Therapy is studied in the traditional way started by Isadore From.

Peter Philippson

Peter Philippson trained as a gestalt Therapist in Great Britain and is a founding member of the Manchester Gestalt Centre. He joined the New York Institute in the early 1990s and became a Full Member a couple of years later. Together with Spagnuolo Lobb, he was one of the first international Full Members.

Erving Polster

Erving Polster is one of the founders of the Cleveland Institute— chronologically, the second gestalt institute and the first institute with a classical training structure. He and his wife Miriam Polster wrote a seminal book *Gestalt Therapy Integrated*. He was trained by Fritz Perls, Isadore From, Paul Weisz, and Paul Goodman. One of his main interests is the application of gestalt therapy theory to work with groups and communities. His account of the Cleveland Institute was important in order to provide a contrast to the New York group.

Margherita Spagnuolo Lobb

Margherita Spagnuolo Lobb is the founder of the Istituto di Gestalt HCC Italy, past President of the European Association for Gestalt Therapy, and one of the first Full Members of the New York Institute from abroad. She came to the institute via Isadore From, who was her therapist and trainer. After From's death in 1994, she worked closely with other NY-IGT's members, such as Richard Kitzler, Dan Bloom, Ruella Frank, and Carl Hodges. Thanks to her, there is a strong communal and theoretical connection between the New York Institute and the Istituto di Gestalt HCC Italy.

Adam Weitz

Adam Weitz was the most recent, and also the youngest, President that I interviewed. His presidential term was from 2017 to 2019. Weitz joined the institute through Susan Gregory, who was initially his therapist. He later joined Identity House where he worked first as a counselor and then as a supervisor. Weitz provided an invaluable insight into the most recent themes occurring in the New York Institute community.

Lee Zevy

Lee Zevy is a Fellow of the NYIGT and served two two-year presidential terms. The first one in 1999 and the second one in 2013. Zevy played an important role in the history of the institute as she was one of the women who participated in the institute's women's caucus (discussed in Chapter 4). She was also a founding member of Identity House. There she met Karen Humphrey and Patrick Kelley, both Fellows of the Institute through whom she joined the institute, going into training with Kelley and Richard Kitzler. In the interviews, she provides a detailed look at the interconnections between the institute and Identity House, the role of feminism, and other historical and cultural aspects of the institute.

Bibliography

Bloom, D. (2019). Interviewed on March 6, 2019.
Wysong, J., & Rosenfeld, E. (1988). *An oral history of gestalt therapy.* The Gestalt Journal Press, Inc.

Chapter 1

Aggressive Attitude

A frequent word used to describe the atmosphere at the monthly institute meetings was "scary!" Especially when we talked about the meetings that took place before the women-led changes (described in Chapter 4) in the early 1990s. But before these changes shifted the institute toward a more inclusive and welcoming atmosphere, the meetings had been a place of argument, aggressiveness, contention, and one-upmanship. In this chapter, I take a close look at this aggressive attitude and bring it into a wider context which includes gestalt therapy theory, the culture among intellectuals in post-war New York, and the social mixture and composition at the institute. In order to better understand the role of gestalt therapy theory, which after all builds on the theory of dental aggression, I take an excursion to the Cleveland Institute where there was a very different atmosphere among the members. I hope that this short detour will provide some contrast to the story of the New York Institute and thus shed some light on the matter.

Monthly Meetings

The monthly institute meetings were often the very first thing mentioned in the interviews. Some called them traumatic and having repercussions on them until today. Perry Klepner, for one, acknowledges that even though there is a different culture at the institute now, he still feels anxious before he is going to give a presentation and ascribes this anxiety to his experience from the early days. In the "old days" fierce critique was not unusual. Even invited guests were subject to frank negative disagreement. The reputation of the institute in this respect was well known. Accomplished and self-confident gestalt therapists, like Joel Latner, were scared to present there (Klepner, 2019). Klepner recalled that he witnessed how an art therapist was dismissed by Isadore From asking her: "You call this gestalt therapy?!" (Klepner, 2019).

The monthly meetings were a part and parcel of the institute life and place for the whole of the institute to meet. The institute members would gather at Laura Perls's apartment or at the community center of a church

DOI: 10.4324/9781003296539-2

in Manhattan. Or somewhere else because even today the institute does not have a fixed address and it is simply there where the members choose to meet. Besides the monthly meetings there were also smaller training groups that met weekly. These first training groups were led by Fritz and Laura Perls, then by Isadore From, Paul Goodman, Richard Kitzler, and others. This structure—of large monthly meetings and the smaller training groups—functioned for a couple of decades but then the latter disappeared. According to those interviewed, it was the training groups where the bonding happened. It was there where people shared their stories, laughed and cried together. After the fiery monthly meetings, people would meet in their training groups and discuss and process their experiences. Belonging to these smaller groups was therefore an important source of support during the peak times of aggressiveness and one-upmanship at the large meetings.

Elinor Greenberg gives a pointed account, which is worth quoting at length, of what it was like for her to experience the meeting for the first time:

GREENBERG: I came to my first New York Institute meeting from my trainer who was only an associate member and his name was Marvin Lifschitz and Marvin was a doll. He was really good, he was a trainer, a kind man, generous and non-competitive. One day he says:

> You're training to be gestalt therapists, you have to go the New York Institute for at least one meeting. And you're probably not going to like it. So, I'll tell you what you gonna expect because every meeting pretty much has the same format. You gonna go, we gonna get to Laura Perls's house, she'll have some cookies out, people will be sitting in the living room, the men will be talking competitively about theory and trying to outdo each other and there will be a lot of people who are too scared to talk and then someone will eventually stand up and say: I'm unclear on how you become a Full Member here and I'd like to become a Full Member; and then there will be silence and everyone will look at her like she's crazy until she sits down and she will never get a straight answer and she will be humiliated and find her seat and that's how it's going to go. So are you prepared? We said: "OK, we're going to go to this strange place as a group." So that was my first meeting and it was just like that. Doug Davidoff was there, I think he's dead now, and he was rather narcissistic and competitive and some other people were there, and they were... whatever they were doing was of no interest to me. It was like going on safari somewhere. And then this woman, who I later became friends with, who wasn't politically astute, stood up and she asked *the* question "how do I become a Full Member?" People looked at her with glances ranging from pity to contempt. She didn't get an answer and so she sat down. And that's how the first meeting went (Greenberg, 2019).

And here is Ruella Frank recalling experience her from the meetings:

FRANK: When I went to the institute, there were very big meetings and people were very forthcoming. It was a little scary for me. Sometimes Isadore [From] would come in and scream and then leave. Others were so
passionate in their points of view. So I never said anything at the institute for about seventeen years because I was too shy to come forward.
[...]
I once presented my work about the fundamental movements as primary supports for contacting. And I started off—which was a mistake—
with the pattern of reaching with the mouth. This was from a chapter I
was working on for my dissertation. We had maybe 35 people at the meeting, and I had them start reaching around the room with their mouths,
as if this was the whole of their experience. Well, it was too much. Many
were absorbed in their thinking and evaluating, rather than their movements, and they sort of flipped out. Half of the group loved the work and
the other half said *What does this have to do with gestalt therapy!?* They
were a fiery group! After the meeting, I said to Richard [Kitzler]: "there
is a lot of dissension about this!" And he said: "Well, Feldenkreis wasn't
very popular until after he died" (Frank, 2019).

Greenberg's and Frank's accounts are corroborated by the well-known history of the style and culture of the institute in its beginnings; Elliot Shapiro,
one of the members of the first training group that was led by Laura Perls and
that was to become the core of the institute, describes the meetings like this:

The original group met consistently for two years. We hammered at
each other, hammered, and hammered—every week. And it was the
most vigorous hammering you can imagine. I recall a friend [...] who
was interested in perhaps moving into psychotherapy on a professional
level. He came to one of the meetings and when he left he spoke to our
mutual friend [...] He said he had never witnessed the aggressive and
profound battling that went on in those groups. Nobody, virtually nobody, was safe at any time.

(Wysong & Rosenfeld, 1988, 79)

Part of the problem, as Bud Feder recalls, was that Richard Kitzler and
Isadore From had a very competitive relationship and they carried out their
fights at the meetings where the younger and less experienced members were
taking the blows for their mentors:

The two of them hated each other and for a long time they dominated
the monthly meetings. I remember I was terrified. I wouldn't say a
word. Because whoever spoke, if Isadore knew you were training under

Richard or Richard knew you were training under Isadore, they just cut you off at the knees, you know.

(Feder, 2015)

A video shot at one of such meetings[1] provides an additional illustration of the atmosphere. The short film is titled *Every Novel Is a Case History* and it is a recording of a monthly NYIGT meeting from December 1988. In that year, Laura Perls was still at the institute as the president, the democratizing changes were just about to happen, and the institute was still run autocratically by the Fellows. Similarly, the changes in the meetings culture were not to happen until about two years later. So what this recording shows is one of the meetings of a transitioning institute.

This December meeting, which lasted for 70 minutes, opens with an interesting announcement by Eric Werthman (a chair of the monthly meeting planning committee) pertaining to the upcoming democratizing structural changes at the institute. Werthman informs the members that the Interim Executive Committee will present its suggestions for the restructuring of the institute at the next meeting in January 1989. In a way these are historical moments for the institute.

After Werthman's announcement, Laura Perls takes the floor and starts reading from her essay. Her presentation lasts for approximately 30 minutes after which she opens the round for a discussion. What ensues is quite interesting: Laura remains the central person throughout the rest of the meeting. She has the full attention: from the people present and also from the camera. The members are sitting in a large circle. The camera, which is placed stationary outside of the circle opposite to Laura, pans left and right but comes to rest on Laura again and again. She is obviously in the spotlight in this recording. Also during the discussion, Laura is addressed again and again. There is some interaction among the members but those who speak end up almost invariably looking at Laura after they said their piece. The discussion itself seems rather cerebral and the atmosphere is tense.

At one point, a woman, who was a guest at this meeting and neither a member of the institute nor a gestalt therapist, asks Laura several questions regarding particular novelists. Her voice is shaky and insecure. As other members join in and comment on what she said, she seems to feel not being understood and wanting to "let it pass." At this point, Richard Kitzler jumps in and says firmly: "No, no, we should not let it pass!" Laughter from the group ensues after which Richard Kitzler continues to explain to this guest that the "real question is" what her unfinished business is with those writers and those novels and that she should go back to them to find out. He does not wait for the women's reaction but turns away instead and starts speaking to Laura. The discussion moves on and the guest does not speak for the rest of the meeting.

Elinor Greenberg was also present. In what seems to be an attempt to counter Kitzler's dismissiveness, she spoke in a friendly and welcoming way with this woman. She greeted her and thanked her for speaking and also acknowledges that some of the gestalt jargon might be difficult to understand for a non-gestaltist. Even some 20 years later, the attitude of welcoming was important for Greenberg (2019): "When I decided to come back to the institute [...] I thought what the institute needs is welcoming. So [I said to myself:] I'm going to be radically inclusive and subversively welcoming."

For many, the kind of aggressive behavior that was dominant at the meetings was off-putting and intimidating. Some needed long years before they gathered the courage and enough self-support to speak out at the meetings. Nevertheless, there were also some who were not dissuaded by this challenging style and who even enjoyed it. For example Dan Bloom. His background was law and he was used to aggressive arguments which for him are a way to explore important matters.

BLOOM: In those days, there were a lot of aggressive conversations at the meetings. You may have heard about that. I liked it! I was used to it. Remember, I was a lawyer. I had no trouble with that whatsoever. I grew up in a family where people would argue. I liked arguing. I like the function of arguing to explore. I understand that some of the arguing was vicious. That didn't bother me either. As a lawyer I was used to haranguing. It was not a big deal.

Although he was not intimidated by the arguments and their fierceness, Bloom admits that he would occasionally feel threatened for a different reason:

BLOOM: I was very new. I didn't know anything clinically. I didn't know any psychological theory whatsoever. I was threatened by all of these people who distrusted anything intellectual, who distrusted any thinking, any thought. I was not one of these human potential oriented people. I was not an Esalen kind of a person. I didn't believe in shouting and screaming. I was put off by that. Not that there were a lot of them there. But that was the general culture of gestalt therapy back in the 1970s. So I was a little wary. I thought I was not likely to be accepted by a lot of gestalt therapists. But the institute itself was also scary, because those were the founders, because those were the people who knew the theory (Bloom, 2019).

Was anything about the aggressive attitude at the monthly meetings a way to live the gestalt therapy theory? Was this "hammering" a kind of a therapeutical exercise? A variant on the experiments from the first part of the *Gestalt Therapy*? Or was it just the way the institute turned out to be—a result of the mix of strong personalities, tough New Yorkers who just love a good altercation, rowdy intellectuals scornful of bourgeois docility, an alienated war generation living the ideal of existentialist authenticity? It will be difficult to find a simple answer to this complex question and probably impossible to untangle all the different strands that lead to the development of this particular style of meetings. However, we can attempt to follow at least some of the strands.

Dental Aggression: Biting through the Flesh

> If you are afraid to hurt people, to attack them, to say "No" when the situation demands it, you should attend to the following exercise: imagine yourself biting a piece of flesh out of someone's body. Can you imagine biting it clean off or do your teeth only make an impression, as if you were biting on rubber?
>
> (Perls, 1992, 236)

If we look at the gestalt therapy theory during the early times of the institute, we can see a strong accentuation of the theory of aggression. It is indeed one of the main theoretical grounds on which this therapeutic modality was built and the New Yorkers were its committed students. The theory of dental aggression was Fritz Perls's original departure from psychoanalysis elaborated in *Ego, Hunger, and Aggression* in 1942. There, aggression is seen as a biological drive on par with Freud's concept of libido. Perls understood psychological processes to be analogical to the organism's food metabolism. The main idea of the theory of dental aggression is the recognition of the organism's active capacity to seek and discriminate in the environment that which is nutritious and to adapt the environment to its own needs. Aggression finds its primary function in chewing of solid food when the teeth develop, but as the organism continues to grow, this drive, as it is called, generalizes into other organismic aspects and functions. Aggression is seen as a required capacity for destruction or deconstruction of unassimilable wholes into parts that can be assimilated or rejected. In a parallel to Freud's theory of repression, Perls considered inhibition in aggression as potentially pathological causing a variety of psychological and societal problems. He therefore argues that aggression should be allowed to follow its natural course for the sake of healthy development:

> Your biological aggressiveness has to find outlets somewhere and somehow; even behind the forgiving character, there lurks a latent aggressive nature which must come out in one way or another, as projection or as moralizing or as killing with kindness. [...] The more we allow ourselves to expend cruelty and lust for destruction in the biologically correct pace — that is, the teeth—the less danger will there be of aggression finding its outlet as a character feature.
>
> (Perls, 1992, 236)

Ten years later, in *Gestalt Therapy: Excitement and Growth in the Human Personality*, aggression is sometimes called drive and other times a contact function. It marks a conceptual shift from the biological emphasis toward the more general phenomenological exploration of contact in the organism/environment field. In the unitary perspective of Perls and Goodman, this changing of names (drive vs contact) is not an inconsistency, it means that aggression finds its expression along the whole continuum of the biological, animal, human, and personal. Though the basic logic of health and pathology remains basically the same, it is now elaborated with a new emphasis on contact:

> The attitude and acts called "aggressive" comprise a cluster of essentially different contact-functions that are usually dynamically interconnected in action and thereby get a common name. We shall try to show that at least annihilating, destroying, initiative, and anger are essential to growth in the organism/environment field; given rational objects, they are always "healthy," and in any case they are irreducible without loss of valuable parts of the personality, especially self-confidence, feeling, and creativity. Other aggressions, like sadomasochism, conquest and domination, and suicide, we shall interpret as neurotic derivates.
>
> (Perls et al., 1994, 120)

We are warned that if aggression is not allowed its proper course as we make contact with our environment, then there will be negative consequences for us. We will lose important capacities in dealing with our lives, in other words, our liveliness will diminish. Freud described the inflictions of repressed sexuality and Perls and Goodman want to show us the fateful effects of inhibited aggression. Their theory of aggression was also their vehicle for a critique of society. In *Gestalt Therapy*, in a section titled *The Antisocial is Presently the Aggressive* we can read:

> The most salient passional characteristics of our epoch are violence and tameness. There are public enemies and public wars unbelievable in scope, intensity, and atmosphere of terror; and at the same time, unexampled civil peace and the almost total suppression of personal outbreaks, with the corresponding neurotic loss of contact, hostility turned against the self, and the somatic symptoms of repressed anger (ulcers, tooth-decay, etc.). [...] Underlying is the inhibited hatred and self-hatred. The deepgoing neurosis, which appears masked in such dreams as comic-books and foreign-policy, is retroflected and projected aggression.
>
> (Perls et al., 1994, 119)

The authors diagnose society with a neurosis of inhibited aggression. Keeping with the psychodynamics of psychoanalysis, the logic here is of a drive: if not allowed to arrive at its objective directly it will take a detour through projections, somatizations, etc. It will turn into a self-hatred if retroflected and if projected it finds devastating outlets in the "good, well-behaved, orderly and infinitely destructive war" (Perls et al., 1994, 119). We can see what the authors suggest as an antidote: the re-integration of aggression into the personal life, its disinhibition in the immediate contact. Their goal is to continue the progress started by psychoanalysis with respect to sexuality and emancipate aggression of the organism in order to prevent its much more destructive projections. How can the authors be sure that the freed aggression will not be too destructive? They rely on the principle of organismic self-regulation, that is, the belief in the organism's social nature and its capacity to regulate its appetites without a need for external control.

Did it work for the institute? Asked whether the aggressiveness at the meetings could be considered as being a technique or used intentionally in order to promote some kind of therapeutic effects envisioned by the theory, Greenberg acknowledged that sometimes it was like that, albeit most of the time it was "bogus" and the only thing that it taught her was how to be cautious around the people at the institute. Also, Klepner recognizes the role of dental aggression in forming the institute's culture but, at the same time, he draws an important distinction between intimidation and aggression:

KLEPNER: We are aggressive now, but one-upmanship is a different kind of aggressiveness and for me it instills a feeling of *I'm not OK*. And one can be aggressive in a healthy way, aggressive and loving, without doing that. By the mid 1980's I remember confronting my mentor Richard Kitzler, telling him that he could be more powerful and impressive with the truth rather than intimidation (Klepner, 2019).

Since our task here is to follow the different strands that lead to the particular style of the institute meetings, we can ask ourselves whether the theory of aggression and, more importantly, the call to its disinhibition may have provided some individuals[2] with a license to be hostile or intimidating. It suggests itself to answer this question in the affirmative. But is there really a way to answer this question in the negative? Can one imagine that these ideas formulated in *Gestalt Therapy*, which the institute elevated to its own blueprint of being,[3] did not encourage some people to go through with their aggressive "drives" and pursue the sharp and bright figure of conflict, because "the achievement of a strong gestalt is itself the cure" (Perls et al., 1994, 8)? What, for example, led Richard Kitzler to be so dismissive to the guest at the above described institute meeting? It is evident that he applies and references gestalt therapy theory in his reaction to that woman when he tells her to read the novels again to find out what her unfinished business is.[4] But why not to give her a chance to react to his statement and take time to explain where his suggestion comes from? It may be that his reaction was a function of his personality, a way for him to secure his position in the group's hierarchy, but would he allow himself this hostility if the theory and the group instead of aggression was emphasizing, for example, empathy?

There is a certain danger when one conceptualizes aggression as a drive. It is a concept that is suggestive of biological energy which requires its outlets one way or another. If the emphasis is one-sidedly biological, then the evoked imagery is one of magma relentlessly pushing toward the surface. It is a phenomenon of nature not of mind or spirit, to use this duality. And because it is biological it is blind to its own consequences. It is also in a sense unavoidable and, as a force of nature, not constructed socially. In order not to fall in this trap of biologism, which can provide simple excuses for any kind of behavior and thus strip an individual of their ethical responsibility, we must understand the aggressive drive as also being shaped by the social self. Klepner uses the words "aggressive *and* loving" to describe the atmosphere at the institute nowadays. These words evoke a more balanced picture somewhat along these lines: we see two people, assertive but open, feelingful but not sentimental, neither fearful of conflict nor abandoning the other.

To be hostile or not is also to some degree a call of moral judgment of which Perls and Goodman had maybe too little to say to counterbalance the weight they gave to undoing the projections and retroflections of aggression. In a short section called *Formation of Personality: Morality*, the authors identify four types of moral evaluations (a) what is good is that kind of behavior that led to success, (b) the norms of a group that one belongs to are seen as good, (c) a new good is discovered in a creative transgression against the old norms, and finally (d):

> The chief cause of confusion is the usual morality of self-conquest: behavior is esteemed as good because of some introjected authority, or it is condemned as bad because one is attacking in oneself the impulse to similar behavior.
>
> (Perls et al., 1994, 204)

Note that there is no mention, for example, of empathy or a concern for the pain of others. But this is not an omission on the part of Perls or Goodman; it expresses the gestalt therapy's optimism with respect to the organism's capacity to self-regulate socially. As Bocian put it:

> The intended result is for individuals increasingly to self-regulate themselves. Through the concept of the organism, they remain inseparably connected with the biological body and the social-environmental field, as opposed to being language and intellect alone. The object is to reduce the introjected "super-ego," balance out one-sided rigid regulation based on morality or reason, and stimulate processual integrative interplay between all human resources.
>
> (Bocian, 2010, 265)

This brings us to an important part of the theory of aggression, namely the theory of introjection and the imperative not to introject.

Never Introject!

The theory of aggression—and with it the theory of health in the organism—stands or falls by the opposition between assimilation and introjection. A healthy growth of the organism, according to Perls and Goodman, depends on continuous assimilation of novelty: the organism seeks in the environment that which is nutritious (physiologically and psychologically), aggresses toward it, de-structures it into assimilable and non-assimilable parts, makes own (identifies with) the former and rejects (alienates) the latter. Introjection is a name for a problematic deviation in this process in which the organism takes in a non-assimilable material. The result is a presence of a so-called *foreign body*[5] which hinders the organism's balanced growth: the parts of the self which are opposed to this foreign body (an introject) have to be continually suppressed and this suppression marks the beginning of a neurosis or, which amounts to the same, the diminishment of awareness of vital parts of the self. When it comes to food it is easy to imagine what an introject, or a foreign element means—a noxious or indigestible matter. The examples of the psychological equivalents are behavioral attitudes, ideas, or societal standards that a person takes for their own although they are in conflict with the person's organismic needs and self-regulation. The remedy against an introjection are, of course, the teeth. Literally and metaphorically: we are to use our aggressive capacity in order not to swallow whole that which should be taken apart. This is also true of the relationships between clients and therapists. The client is not supposed to swallow the therapist's "wisdom" without discrimination. In a way, it was this theory that took the patient out of the couch and placed them on a chair facing and confronting the therapist.[6]

Over time, as gestalt therapy developed different emphases (e.g. relational approach), the concept of introjection lost some of its prominence but at the beginning of gestalt therapy its importance was still paramount. Both Richard Kitzler and Isadore From considered it the corner stone of the theory and Fritz Perls's major achievement. It is a well known saying among gestalt therapists that the founding text was written deliberately in a challenging style so as not be easily introjected; here in words of Isadore From:

> The implication for the writer of a text, and I think Goodman recognized this, was that a serious text could not be written if it risked being introjected by the reader. What we insist on calling the theoretical is a way of writing about this serious matter, Gestalt therapy, in a way that reasonably prevents introjection.
>
> (Wysong & Rosenfeld, 1988, 36)

However, this might as well be a myth and Laura Perls seems to set the record straight. Asked whether Paul Goodman wrote the book on purpose in a style which precludes introjections, she answered laconically: "No, that's just how Paul normally wrote" (Doubrawa & Doubrawa, 2005, 142).[7] But even if it is a myth, it is an informing one and its very existence shows us how vital it was for the New York group to avoid introjection.

Under what condition does introjection happen? Sometimes introjection is presented as a basically painful imposition on the organism. Like in a predicament when neither destruction nor assimilation is possible and the organism is forced to retract its aggression and take in the unwanted material. The authors give an example of a child whose parent, on which it vitally depends, is both a needed and pain-causing object. Other times, introjection seems less painful or less enforced, like when we adopt attitudes and behaviors through imitation of authorities without a "selective and critical attitude toward what is offered [to us]" (Perls et al., 1994, 435). Whether painful or not, the concept of introjection builds on the idea of an essentially healthy (balanced, spontaneous) organism that is confronted with an unhealthy (limiting, coercive, intruding) environment. Often it is the social standards that the authors have in mind when they identify the environment as that which disturbs the organism's lively excitation[8] and spontaneous pursuit of its needs:

> If he cannot identify himself and alienate what is not himself in terms of his own needs, he confronts a void. The social environment contains all the reality there is, and he constitutes himself by identifying with its standards, and alienating what are potentially his own standards.
>
> (Perls et al., 1994, 233)

In some sense, the theory around introjection is a declamation of an anti-authoritarian stance and, as I will discuss in the next section, together with the concept of organismic self-regulation it constitutes Goodman's anarchistic outlook. Here, I want to point to the problematic aspect of this concept: it invites us to discard anything that in some way disturbs our organismic integrity and limits our spontaneity. But anything novel is a priori unknown and therefore disturbing. So, for fear of introjection, I may actually close off my boundaries and thus prevent my own growth. Consider this account given by Perry Klepner:

KLEPNER: I always not liked communications that were off-putting and there were many many emails, even as late as early 2000s, people speaking in terms of "I'm gonna speak the way I speak, I'm gonna speak the way I think is appropriate, not according to any one else." And Kitzler had this also. Kitzler said: "I'm not going to adjust myself to you. If you wanna make contact with me, you gonna have to adjust yourself to me." Fritz did that also, he refused to answer questions and he was very demanding about people. Some of our members still have that. For me—something I learned from Isadore—when I speak to people I do adjust myself; it does not make sense to me to speak to an ear that can't hear me.

Is not the statement "I am going to speak the way I speak, not according to any one else" crude but concise formulation of an anti-introjection stance? There is a touch of juvenile quality in this proclamation, and so it is fitting that Erving and Miriam Polster (1974, 74) identified adolescence, next to the "terrible twos," as the developmental phase par-excellence during which we resist introjection with all the force that we have. Perls's and Goodman's resistance to any kind of introjection is therefore an appeal to our rebellious energies. But there is also a potential for conscienceless egocentrism. The problem is immediately evident when we consider the fact the authors identify conscience as a self-conquest and a result of (pathological) introjection:

> In your own case consider some escapade in which you succeeded and had a good time. Under those circumstances your conscience gave you little trouble; but if you failed, got caught, or were disappointed, then you felt guilty and your conscience told you you should not have done it. Logically we must say that it is the person's anger against the frustrating obstacles—which anger, however, he cannot vent nor even feel as such because of his identification with (introjection of) the social standards—that now he projects into his conscience [...] It is not the introjected standard that gives strength to the conscience; it merely provides the nucleus, the appropriate screen upon which the person may project aggression. [...] The strength of conscience is the strength of one's own reactive anger!
>
> (Perls et al., 1994, 463–464)

In other words, conscience is a conglomerate of un-organic introjects, such as social standards, and its heft comes from the held back resentment which we felt toward those who hindered our ventures. The authors oppose morality based on conscience and favor the ethics based on "the wisdom of the organism":

> Do not be afraid that by dissolving conscience you will become a criminal or an impulsive psychopath. You will be surprised, when you allow organic self-regulation to develop and your outgoing drives to contact other persons, how the principles that you ought to live by will seem to emerge from your very bones and will be obviously appropriate for living out regardless of the social situation you are in.
>
> (Perls et al., 1994, 464)

Their view can be characterized as *immoral ethics* (Žižek, 2013, 124): what matters is "my consistency in relation to myself, my fidelity to my own desire" (ethics) and not "the symmetry of my relations to other humans" (morality).[9]

Organismic Self-Regulation, Ethics, and Social Responsibility

When Perls and Goodman instruct us on how to dissolve our conscience, it is not their intention, of course, to turn us into asocial maniacs but actually the opposite: they want us to realize our social nature. They can make this claim because they conceive of organism as essentially social and locate the source of pathology in an overly restrictive society and its morality based on self-conquest. This antagonism—organism vs society—is one of the basic premises of the theory and is frequently reiterated, like in this excerpt:

> It is [...] the meddling inward of outside-the-skin social forces that deliberately upsets the spontaneous inner-system and calls for psychotherapy.
> (Perls et al., 1994, 135)

The spontaneous inner system is the basis of the organismic self-regulation. When we are aware of our emergent needs and pursue their fulfillment in the environment spontaneously and creatively, plus we do so with a sharp awareness for the actuality of the situation, then we are self-regulating organismically. If, on the other hand, we are overly deliberate, if we do not let our creativity to contact the actuality with an open-minded curiosity, when we hinder our excitement in the face of a novel situation, if our reactions are rigidly habitual, then this kind of self-regulation is called neurotic. Perls and Goodman saw a society caught in a predicament of tame and guilty subordination to authorities and disastrous madness of mass destruction. Organismic self-regulation was their answer to these problems. One can note the whiff of existentialism: the individual's duty to live an authentic life and to suffer its own freedom, but also a touch of optimism: it is equally a life of creativity and excitement. It is also a view that reflects Goodman's anarchistic ideal[10] that a truly livable social order can emerge only out of organismic contacting.

The usual objection against organismic self-regulation makes the point that Perls and Goodman were too focused on the biological/animal side of what it means to be human and overlooked the troublesome aspects of what it means to be also a person with relationships that go beyond mere fulfillment of the currently dominant need. But this critique is not fully justified because the concept of organismic self-regulation encompasses the whole spectrum, from the physical to the biological to the animal to the person:

But there is no such thing as "merely" biological functioning (for instance, there is no such drive as "mere" sex, without either love or the avoidance of love).

(Perls et al., 1994, 86)

[Since] it is meaningful to say that it is by organismic-self-regulation that one imitates, sympathizes, becomes "independent", and can learn arts and sciences, the expression "animal" contact cannot mean "merely" animal contact.

(Perls et al., 1994, 93)

Therefore, in order to bring out the strength of the theory, we have to understand the word "organismic" in this encompassing sense expressing the totality of our being. To put it differently, to self-regulate organismically does not mean to prioritize the biological/animal needs, it means to be fully constituted as a physical-biological-animal-social being.

But is it actually possible to be so fully constituted? What are the limits of this idea? What does it mean with respect to ethics? And how did this concept influence the community at the New York Institute? In order to address these questions, let us contrast organismic self-regulation with a radically different view:

[There is an] irreducible gap between subjective authenticity and moral goodness (in the sense of social responsibility): the difficult thing to accept is that one can be totally authentic in overcoming one's false Self and yet still commit horrible crimes—and vice versa, of course: one can be a caring subject, morally committed to the full, while existing in an inauthentic world of illusion with regard to oneself. [...] In order to be fully engaged ethico-politically, it is necessary to exit the "inner peace" of one's subjective authenticity.

(Žižek, 2013, 135)

Now, one could argue that authenticity and organismic self-regulation are not the same thing,[11] but that is not the point here. What is important is that in Perls's and Goodman's framework of thought, there is practically no place for the idea that one has to leave the "inner peace" of organismic self-regulation in order to be ethical in a sense that goes beyond the spontaneous hierarchy of the organisms' needs. At one point, the authors acknowledge that we have to make certain concessions, but they also lament the loss of spontaneity:

This is the case even when self-regulation is inhibited in the obvious interests of the self: e.g., when a child is kept from running in front of automobiles, a situation in which his self-regulation is fallible — and the way we run our societies seems to consist largely of such situations. The inhibition then is necessary, but let us remember that to the extent to which we agree to situations in which self-regulation rarely operates, to that extent we must be content to live with diminished energy and brightness.

(Perls et al., 1994, 52–53)

Do we then have to become neurotic in order to also be socially responsible? To answer this question in the affirmative would of course be problematic for the theory of Perls and Goodman. In a rare moment of self-doubt, they actually do consider this possibility when they discuss the anthropology of neurotic conflicts:

[It] is also likely that these [...] "irreconcilable" conflicts have always been, not only at present, the human condition; and that the attendant suffering and motion toward an unknown solution are the grounds of human excitement.

(Perls et al., 1994, 96)

In other words, humanity is condemned to a perpetual circling around its own neuroses for the sake of pleasure and pain. This is an interesting thought, Lacanian[12] in a way, but it goes counter to the usual optimism of gestalt therapy theory. Obviously, Perls and Goodman do not pursue it and their theoretical edifice stands on other assumptions: (1) that the organismic self-regulation is achievable and (2) that a good contact with the actuality of the situation is in itself a guarantee for a good communal outcome. These two premises express the belief that our needs and the needs of society are mutually compatible and can coexist in a non-neurotic field. In a way it is a utopian vision and their book, *Gestalt Therapy*, is its manifesto. What becomes evident when we contrast the view expressed by Žižek with that of Perls and Goodman is that the organismic self-regulation is fundamentally a hopeful concept. In other words, there is a part of us that is not "corrupted" by society and on which we can rely. And, indeed, this is what the authors state explicitly:

[S]ocial pressures do not deform organismic-self-regulation that is "good" and "not anti-social" when it is properly understood and said with the acceptable words; society forbids what is destructive of society. There is not a semantical mistake but a genuine conflict.

(Perls et al., 1994, 116)

Perls and Goodman, of course, recognize that the organismic self-regulation can be hindered—that is their theory of neurosis—but it is basically available, it operates somewhere in us and by increasing our awareness, we can eventually reach it. We can imagine the opposing view, the pessimistic and skeptical one: though achievable the organismic self-regulation is not good per se. The spontaneous emergence of needs, as a true phenomenon of the field, is "contaminated" by the antagonisms of society. It is pessimistic in the sense that we do not have any guarantee of a good outcome and it is skeptical because we cannot fully trust our own needs.

When it comes to the problem of ethics and social responsibility, the pessimistic view does not try to bridge the "irreducible gap" and so it leaves us caught in it. It tells us that we have nothing to rely on in our ethical choices except our fallible and neurotic means. There is no good organismic self-regulation to save us. To put it differently, there are no a priori criteria, aesthetic, theoretical, or otherwise, that could help us in our predicament. It suggests, that in order to be *socially responsible*, we cannot let ourselves be guided solely by what *feels* organismic to us. To some limited degree, this is true also in the optimistic view. There are instances where, for the sake of not only social responsibility but also of personal growth, we have to go against that what we experience as our organic, natural way. Probably all our neurotic defenses fall into that category; when in therapy, we walk our reaction formation back to the source of pain; we move in a sense against ourselves, against our instincts. In other words, given that our starting point is a neurotic situation, we have a good reason to scrutinize that which emerges spontaneously.

What does this mean for the New York Institute? Can it be that the optimism of organismic self-regulation supported a culture which prioritized spontaneity and conflict thus pushing into background the less loud aspects of contacting? Would the climate at the meetings be different if this foundational concept did not try to provide a guarantee for a good communal outcome? And if it were not so hopeful, would then the resulting skepticism make the members more cautious in their pursuit of the bright and strong figures of conflict? And what good would be lost in this process? For sure, Paul Goodman's "anarchism, utopianism, and Gandhianism" (Goodman, 1991, 219) would count among the losses. Would some of the liveliness and excitement, too? From another angle, the problem of ethics and social responsibility is also a question of where on the continuum between the individual and the communal our attention goes and how flexibly can it move from one to the other. It is a fact that the institute started with a strong focus on the individual. In Chapters 4 and 5, I will describe how this focus gradually shifted toward the explorations of group dynamics and the field conditions and how it changed the culture at the institute.

Lost Homes; New Family

Both Klepner and Greenberg see also other reasons for the hostilities at the meetings. Not the application of the theory but the culture in the postwar New York and the dominant personality-style of the institute. In other words, the particular style at the meetings is seen as carrying on with the founding figures' heritage.

KLEPNER: In my view, the New York Institute has a long history of evolution. Beginning with the founding by Fritz and Laura Perls and the attitudes and ideas they brought to it. Fritz was a wonderful innovator and creative spirit and Laura was very stable. They founded the institute essentially to create a teaching program so they could have students and make a living here in New York. They gathered around them a very smart, liberal, and informed group including Paul Goodman and Paul Weisz and the others that they had with them. [...] The book was published in 1951, the institute was founded in 1952. But there is a very aggressive attitude they all seem to have that came from the post World War II period, and probably was sourced even prior to that, of competitiveness and one-upmanship and they would aggressively critique the theory that Perls was presenting and that Goodman had [written]. These were strong people who set the tone for the institute.

GREENBERG: When we would have inter-institute meetings with other institutes, like we do at a conference, they would all hug each other in a group from the institutes, our group could barely stand each other. Our group was awkward. I used to think of ourselves as the schizoid institute, the schizoid-narcissist institute. Half the people were putting you down so you keep your distance, the other half were putting you down so they can feel better. And despite Laura being involved it was very masculine. [...] Every so often I would come to a meeting and because they remained modeled after the very first meeting there was always somebody being humiliated and I really didn't like that.

If modernity signified a break with tradition, then the two World Wars were the deafening bangs announcing the collapse. The result was a traumatized world with a ruptured and emptied horizon. What now after all this destruction? And what to do with all the feelings of alienation? The void was a wound but also vibrant in possibilities. The vacant space was quickly being filled with heated creativity in arts, sciences, and technology, eventually cooling off in the supernova-like nebula of postmodernity. In philosophy, it was existentialism that sprang out of the turmoils. Confronting the hypocrisy of society, existentialists called for the individual to live authentically and seize its freedom and responsibility. They had seen where the conventional morality had led humanity to. Not so much the extreme of an enforced submission but the everyday, "normal" obedience to the authorities was seen as the cause of the problems (Arendt's banality of evil) and the authentic individual was to be the new foundation of society. This idea carried all the hope for a sensible social arrangement and Laura and Fritz Perls were its proponents. The liberal circles that they gathered around them shared their vision and it made its imprint on the functioning of the community which eyed with fierce suspicion anything that remotely looked like conformism.

When we want to follow the strand of the "family heritage" and understand the communal culture at the institute from this perspective, then we have to also keep in mind that gestalt therapy was born in this post-destruction process of coming into terms with a trauma and losses. And among these losses, one of the most prominent one was the loss of home. Bernd Bocian in his book *Fritz Perls in Berlin*, which follows Perls's life and intellectual development up to the point of his and his wife's escape from Nazi Germany, writes with great sensitivity and understanding of this connection between uprootedness and gestalt therapy:

> I propose that Perls's topicality is based on the life experiences and, above all, the *survival experiences* of the exiled European-German urban avant-garde, which entered into the therapeutic approach that his contributions shaped so fundamentally.
>
> (Bocian, 2010, 249)

Bocian points out that the home that was left, was left for good. There was no possibility of returning—the loss was final, the damage was irreversible. The resulting emptiness created the need to build new homes and connections. But on what foundations when the very idea of stability was shattered? A sentimental attempt to re-create what was lost in the past was not an option for the liberal and progressive intellectuals of the "lost generation." So they had to create and establish novel conditions in the flux of their actuality:

> The representatives of the cultural avant-garde and the creative Expressionist spirit often viewed themselves as cosmopolitans, citizens of the world, whereas in reality they were generally "citizens without a world" so to speak. It was only in a self-constructed counter or parallel culture that they found an opportunity to create a place of belonging, where they then usually attempted to »be free within their connectedness« to other like-minded spirits, as Erich Mühsam once put it. After their human and social ideals had been destroyed by the events of 1914 and 1933, they found their "true homeland" in exile.
>
> (Bocian, 2010, 267)

Besides Laura and Fritz Perls, there were others at the New York Institute who also had an urgent need to find new connections and sense of belonging, albeit in a different sense. As I will discuss in detail in the next chapter, the institute became a vitally important place for people from the LGBT community. Under the influence of Paul Goodman and others the institute was the only institute of the time that welcomed gays, lesbians, and bisexuals and for many of them, it became a second home. Lee Zevy pointed out how coming out as a homosexual often meant a disruption of family ties, sometime to the point of an actual loss of the family of origin so that for some the institute was life-saving. And even if the family ties survived more or less intact, the wider society was never so generous. Paul Goodman, who lived his bisexuality openly and unapologetically, impresses upon us with just a few words the trauma of rejection:

> I don't complain that my passes are not accepted; nobody has a claim to be loved (except small children). But I am degraded for making the passes at all, for being myself. Nobody likes to be rejected, but there is a way of rejecting someone that accords him his right to exist and is the next best thing to accepting him. I have rarely enjoyed this treatment.
>
> (Goodman, 1991, 216)

And after he lists the three occasions on which he lost his job, an account of being bisexual—jobs at "highly liberal and progressive institutions, and two of them prided themselves on being communities"—he concludes with brutal frankness: "Nevertheless, I am all for community because it is a human thing, only I seem doomed to be left out" (Goodman, 1991, 217). And yet, the New York Institute, which Paul Goodman had helped to establish, became for many non-heterosexual people this longed for community:

> ZEVY: The community was not only social, collegial and friends. It's all in one. They are family, actually. [...] To a large extent, they became more important in certain ways than our families of origin (Zevy, 2019).

And others whom I interviewed also used the words family and home to describe what they found at the institute. Many of the second and third generation of members were the pariahs of their families and the mainstream, heteronormative society. So they too, in a sense, lost a world and lived in an exile. In the 1980s, there was another trauma that hit the New York Institute. The community was losing loved people to AIDS. Breathing heavily, Dan Bloom answers my question how these losses affected the institute:

> BLOOM: In a way it's hard to even know because I was so much in the middle of it. It really influenced us. I don't know how many people who were members died. I think it was about five. We were very much involved in the fight against AIDS. [...] We had presentations about death and dying. One of my teachers, Patrick Kelly died of AIDS. That really hurt us (Bloom, 2019).

Perhaps, one more way to understand the aggressive attitude at the New York Institute is to see it against the background of these losses and the need to defend this newly found community, identity, and sense of belonging. The theory, which brought the people together, was not just an abstract and neutral academic matter, a mere scholastic interest. Lives depended on it intimately. So, when Isadore From used his favorite and feared sentence, "And you call this gestalt therapy?!" was he not protecting something of vital importance for him and others? Greenberg saw narcissistic and schizoid defenses in the community at the institute and in a broad sense we can maybe understand them as creative adjustments to the lack of acceptance and attunement in society.

Cleveland for Comparison

In order to better understand the role of the theory on the culture of the New York Institute, we should look at the institute in Cleveland for comparison. The institute in Cleveland, where Erving and Miriam Polster were two of the chief figures, formed already in 1954 as a learning community; about ten years later, the institute also started providing formal gestalt therapy training. Fritz Perls, Laura Perls, Paul Goodman, Paul Weisz, and Isadore From were the first trainers who went to Cleveland and presented gestalt therapy. While the Perls and the two Pauls were occasional guest trainers who used to come a couple of times per year to offer a workshop or a course, Isadore From was the one who came regularly and did individual therapy with the Cleveland group. He recalled:

> [Fritz Perls] informed these people that I would be coming there. That made me uneasy. First of all, most of these people were very well-trained psychologists—all of them. Why should they take me, whose background was quite different than theirs, and take me on the order of Perls? And they did. But I made it quite clear that this was on a trial basis. That lasted 5 years, twice a month—and then 5 more years, once a month, and at least once or twice a year since then.
>
> (Wysong & Rosenfeld, 1988, 35)

Besides being the therapist of the group, Isadore From also led the theoretical seminars and as in the New York Institute, the text of *Gestalt Therapy* was approached in a gestalt-specific way. It was read line by line, out loud in a group and discussed; any difficulty in understanding the material was considered first and foremost as a difficulty on the part of the reader whose fixed character stood in the way of the understanding of the text.[13] Even nowadays the text is taught in this way. Klepner, for example, offers online groups that meet once a month, where the text is read in this traditional, slow, and careful way, each paragraph or so followed by a discussion by the whole group.

From the very beginning, the atmosphere in the Cleveland group was very different from the one at the New York Institute. The original group had

15 members who knew each other from before, mostly through university. They were graduates of psychology and were interested in the new developments. Some of them trained originally in psychoanalysis and the novelty of gestalt therapy fascinated them. Gestalt therapy represented a new way of looking at life and of being open to personal experience. They organized themselves and invited the New Yorkers to come and teach them. Erving Polster recalled that the Cleveland group was a collective of compatible, warm, good-hearted people and their leaderless weekly meetings had a feeling of holidays (Polster, 2019). The New Yorkers feared their meetings while the Clevelanders enjoyed each other's company like good friends. How is such a gaping difference possible and how can it be accounted for?

What the Cleveland example shows us is that the role of the theory on the culture of the community must not be overstated and we should search for its proper place and explore its constitutive role in a wider context. The views of Klepner and Greenberg, that there was a certain culture or group personality prior to the theory which contributed to the contentious atmosphere at the institute meetings, seem justified. So instead of looking for a rather naive direct causation (e.g. a theory of dental aggression is the reason for the aggressive attitudes), we must reframe the question and try to understand the community and the theory as field phenomena in interaction: the theory is the expression of the culture/personality and the culture/personality is the expression of the theory; in an evolving feedback loop, the community accentuates certain theoretical aspects which then influence the organization of the community itself.

Isadore From was known for the close attention he paid to the theory and given the importance he ascribed to the concept of introjection (intrinsically linked to the theory of dental aggression), it is unlikely that the Cleveland group would not get familiar with the theoretical parts dealing with aggression. It is much more likely that the Cleveland group, by the nature of its composition, did not accentuate these parts in the way the New Yorkers did.

In 1973, Erving and Miriam Polsters published their seminal book *Gestalt Therapy Integrated* (dedicated to Isadore From, the "teacher and friend"), which attempted to provide a coherent account of gestalt therapy and praxis. It was a successful book which became part and parcel of the theoretical canon taught at the gestalt institutes worldwide. The take on gestalt therapy presented there can be considered the Cleveland model. The book is written in an accessible style and, in contrast to Perls's and Goodman's work, it does not try so hard to cut the cord from Freud but presents gestalt therapy in a self-confident, clear, and coherent way. Additionally, the book has a clear-cut scope; its aim is to describe a new psychotherapeutic modality, and so we do not find almost any of the social criticism and a more general outlook as we do in *Gestalt Therapy*. All in all, it is an easy-to-read and practical book.

The topic of aggression, which is not to be found in the index of this book, is subsumed in the short section on introjection and even though the concept of dental aggression is referenced, it does not acquire the importance and dimensions as it did in *Gestalt Therapy*. There, as I have pointed out above, it was central to the author's social diagnosis and seen as underdeveloped and complementary polarity to sexuality, which was already emancipated by psychoanalysis. We do not find any such sociological generalizations in *Gestalt Therapy Integrated*. Polsters's view does not emphasize aggression but places it as equal among other contact functions of the organism. In a way, their book makes an impression of an intermediary between Fritz Perls's *Gestalt Therapy Verbatim*—which was published some four years prior to their book—*Gestalt Therapy*. It attempts a formulation of a coherent theory but integrates also to some degree Fritz Perls's intuitive and exuberant therapeutic style.[14]

One of the frequent critiques heard of the address of the so-called West Coast style of gestalt therapy was that some of Perls's followers lacked erudition. While Fritz Perls's decades of working as a psychoanalyst informed his dramatic working style, those that copied him did not have his experience, his vast assimilated knowledge, and his virtuosity; they—so the critique goes—merely emulated the spectacular parts of Perls's work without the deeper background and thus they were occasionally causing damage to patients. Isadore From's scathing remarks with respect to the developments on the West Coast are telling:

> I never use the word gestalt without the word therapy. Through a curious development we began a gestalt therapy and somewhere on one of the coasts of this continent the word therapy was dropped and something known as gestalt emerged. They probably correctly dropped the word therapy.
>
> (Weaver, 2019)

However, the people in Cleveland were no Perls's copycats and Fritz was not their sole teacher. Moreover, they were all well-trained psychologists who could stand their ground and who in the end developed their own version of gestalt therapy. The Cleveland people saw some shortcomings of gestalt therapy and offered some corrections, for example, with regard to working with groups and communities. According to Erving Polster, one of the problems of the image of gestalt therapy then was its emphasis on immediacy and honesty without consideration for the context. This emphasis was new and inspiring but it also failed to consider what people could do at a particular time (Polster, 2019). The attempt at straight-on talk could become quickly intimidating when the timing was disregarded. This judgment call—when to say what—was lost in the radical emphasis on immediacy and Polsters's *Gestalt Therapy Integrated* addressed these issues (albeit more implicitly in style rather than stated explicitly). According to Erving Polster, the Cleveland group's special flavor of gestalt therapy was the quality of live and let live. He then elaborated: "It's a matter of recognizing that the only way to have a community is to be able to coordinate independence with belonging" (Polster, 2019).

It seems that the Cleveland group provided the landscape of gestalt therapy with a moderate climate: they were "a group of friendly, warm, and good-hearted people" (Polster, 2019), and some of them knew each other from the university. They were professionals who were interested in learning a new modality. They eventually created a gestalt institute with a traditional structure, with faculty members and with a curriculum. Students came, graduated, received their certificates, and then they moved on. The community of the Cleveland institute was predominantly the community of the faculty staff and not as in the case of the New York Institute a wide ranging assortment of therapists, trainees, patients, or occasional visitors.

In the search for the reasons why the Cleveland group enjoyed each other's company to the degree that their meetings would have a feeling of holidays whereas the New Yorkers would occasionally leave their meetings pained and wounded, several striking differences between the two groups emerge. These differences pertain to the composition of the group, the purpose of the group, the stage of development of gestalt therapy theory, and its accentuation.

Composition of the Group

The New York Institute brought together a mixed group of people. Only some, like Elliot Shapiro or Richard Kitzler, where psychologists, others came from different walks of life. Paul Goodman, for example, was a writer and Isadore From studied social research. Additionally, the New York Institutes' open and non-pathologizing attitude toward homosexuals attracted many who identified as such. This open attitude was radical in the 1950s' America and this spirit of radicalness (perfectly embodied by Paul Goodman himself) was present at the New York Institute. The Cleveland group was quite different in this respect—more homogeneous. It was originally formed by people who have graduated from Western Reserve University in psychology and their main motivation was their professional advancement, rather than a personal need, like in the case of many of the New York people.

The Purpose of the Group

Fritz, with help of Laura Perls, developed a new therapeutic method, wanted to establish it, and the original New York group was their vehicle to do it. People were selected as patients when they also had a utility for this purpose like in the case of Isadore From. He sought Fritz Perls for the sake of psychotherapy in times of a personal crisis. Initially, Perls refused to take him as a patient because From could not afford his fee. However, when From mentioned that he studied Husserl's phenomenology, Perls agreed to work with him (Wysong & Rosenfeld, 1988, 27). Whereas the New York group formed out of Laura's and Fritz's patients, the Cleveland group formed out of peers with a common interest. Their goal, at least initially, was not to promote or develop gestalt therapy; they came together to learn it and only later as they became proficient did they start to teach it and elaborate on it.

The Stage of Gestalt Therapy Theory

Fritz and Laura Perls came to New York around 1947. At that time, they still called themselves psychoanalysts. That changed only after the publication of *Gestalt Therapy* that established this modality. It was published in 1951, a year before the New York Institute was formally established. Goodman was originally hired as an editor for the texts supplied by Fritz Perls but as Laura Perls relates, he contributed so much to the theory that he became a coauthor. In fact, according to Laura, there would not be a coherent gestalt therapy theory without Paul Goodman (Wysong & Rosenfeld, 1988, 13). The Cleveland group formed in 1954 and started to offer training in 1966. We can see that these two groups emerged at different stages of the development of the modality. The New York group experienced the creative efforts of formulating and establishing the theory while the Cleveland group were already learners of an albeit fresh but considerably complete therapeutic school.

Accentuation of the Theory

Aggression and the undesirability of introjection were of utmost concern for the early New York group. The Cleveland group, however, did not have this theoretical focus. This distinction is clearly seen by the comparison of the institutes' respective major theoretical outputs: *Gestalt Therapy* by Perls, Hefferline, and Goodman on one hand and *Gestalt Therapy Integrated* by Erving and Miriam Polster on the other. A simple heuristic can be useful to understand how the accentuation in the theory shifted: using the index entries, I have identified seven strongest[15] keywords in each book. In *Gestalt Therapy*, these are: Freud, contact, self, introjection, psychoanalysis, therapy, and aggression. And in *Gestalt Therapy Integrated*: contact episodes, contact, experience, group interactions, unfinished business, I-boundaries, and awareness. I admit I like the fact that in the work of Perls, Hefferline, and Goodman, the honorable first place is Freud's. It is a reminder of where gestalt therapy comes from but also of the tremendous creative effort (and chutzpah) of Perls and Goodman to establish an original school of psychotherapy next to the towering presence of psychoanalysis. Then there is the "holy quaternity" of self, contact, introjection, and aggression, which must be probably the most concise answer to the question *What is the theory of Perls and Goodman?* In the case of the Cleveland institute, the focus is on experiencing, contacting, and awareness. The expression *unfinished business* comes from the vocabulary of the so-called West Coast style—though as unfinished situation it appears also in the book by Perls and Goodman—and so it points to the aforementioned integration of the different approaches. And there is also the Cleveland Institute's specific theoretical interest in groups and community which chronologically preceded Fritz Perls's and the New York Institute's. On account of Perls's later interest in gestalt communities, Erving Polster comments:

POLSTER: When I started working on communal things, Fritz pooh-poohed it and the next thing I know he was in Vancouver![16] Actually, he had one [gestalt community] before that in Taos, New Mexico. He was a man who would be a center-piece in a community but he was not going to be a communal engager (Polster, 2019).

A Remark

This chapter may have created an impression that the New York Institute for gestalt therapy was a troubled place where people got hurt. This impression is not incorrect, but one has to complete the picture with other important aspects of the community. For many, the institute is something close to a family and in the next chapters, I elaborate on this topic. The bonding that developed among the peers proved to be solid and lasting.

Many of the people I interviewed stayed committed to the institute over decades until this day. They also volunteered for various administrative positions, be it the presidency or serving as a secretary or a treasurer. These functions usually mean a significant amount of unpaid work. Besides that, they were active in various committees thus supporting the institute's ongoing development. I was repeatedly impressed by the level of commitment, engagement, and caring for the institute that I could witness by listening to their stories. Some of my interview partners were deeply appreciative for what they found there. Perry Klepner, for one, described it as "life giving" (Klepner, 2019).

The New York community grappled with its tradition of aggression for many years. Around the 1990s, the institute underwent a transformation structurally and culturally. The changes were an attempt to deal among other things along with this heritage. They were to a large degree successful and I describe them in Chapters 4 and 5. But some strands of this defining specter of the institute are still active today and to come to terms with them is an ongoing effort. Adam Weitz offers a perspective of a younger generation and recalls how one of the new members confessed to him that the current large meetings feel like listening to the older relatives argue. He acknowledges that this is a quite an accurate description but adds that the arguments—theoretical and personal—are rich and intriguing. They go on between people who have a long history together and one can occasionally sense the connection and love they have for each other.

Notes

1 Available at Institute's homepage (newyorkgestalt.org/media/videos).
2 It would be more precise to say *male individuals*, since it was mainly the men that behaved this way. This strand of male/female polarity and conflict is followed in detail in Chapter 4 where I discuss the feminist revolution at the institute.
3 As I have already quoted Bloom: "People gathered around learning and teaching and they lived the theory with one another."
4 He bases his reprimand on the contextual method of argument described in *Gestalt Therapy*. The idea behind this hermeneutical method is "to bring into the picture the total context of the problem, including the conditions of experiencing it, the social milieu and the personal 'defenses' of the observer" (Perls et al., 1994, 20). This was also the way the founding book was read and interpreted at the institute. Isadore From used this method in his training groups:

> Not that I insisted that they take the text as holy writ, but it was interesting to assume that a difficulty of understanding, when reading the text, might be the difficulty of the reader and that might be worth working through. Then we could also criticize the text.
>
> (Wysong & Rosenfeld, 1988, 35)

5 The wording "foreign body" is taken directly from *Gestalt Therapy*:

> An introject [...] consists of material—a way of acting, feeling, evaluating— which you have taken into your system of behavior, but which you have not assimilated in such fashion as to make it a genuine part of your organism. You took it in on the basis of a forced acceptance, a forced (and therefore pseudo-) identification, so that, even though you will now resist its dislodgment as if it were something precious, it is actually a foreign body.
>
> (Perls et al., 1994, 433)

6 One could venture further and say that it was the importance of empathy that achieved the same shift from a couch to a chair for the Rogerians. The differences here can also be illuminating: whereas gestalt therapy tries to bring forth the creative, aggressive and spontaneous capacity of the self, the person-centered therapy supports the development of a person's congruent self-image.
7 Taylor Stoehr (2009) discovered that at one point, Goodman's style of writing received scorn from George Orwell who used it as an exhibit three in his essay *Politics and the English* Language (Orwell, 1946). Susan Sontag, on the other hand, admired his style and was more generous to some of Goodman's stylistic idiosyncrasy:

> Paul Goodman's voice is the real thing. There has not been such a convincing, genuine, singular voice in our language since D.H. Lawrence. Paul Goodman's voice touched everything he wrote about with intensity, interest, and his own terribly appealing sureness and awkwardness. What he wrote was a nervy mixture of syntactical stiffness and verbal felicity; he was capable of writing sentences of a wonderful purity of style and vivacity of language, and also capable of writing so sloppily and clumsily that one imagined he must be doing it on purpose. But it never mattered. It was his voice, that is to say, his intelligence and the poetry of his intelligence incarnated, which kept me a loyal and passionate addict. Though he was not often graceful as a writer, his writing and his mind were touched with grace.
>
> (Goodman, 2012, 275–276)

8 In the words of the authors:

> The neurotic situation is that in which the convention is coercive and incompatible with a lively excitation, and where in order to avoid the offense of not belonging (not the speak of further conflicts), the desire itself is inhibited and the hateful environment is both annihilated and accepted by swallowing it whole and blotting it out.
>
> (Perls et al., 1994, 233).

9 Žižek uses the term immoral ethics to describe Nietzsche's theory of morality. Perls and Goodman, too, reference Nietzsche when they discuss morality based on introjection as resentment and self-conquest.

10 Aylward (2014, 394) about Goodman: "From a political perspective, the gestalt principle of 'organismic self-regulation' morphs quite comfortably into his anarchistic orientation since self-sufficiency inherently requires little in the way of external control of any sort."

11 Whether they are the same or not depends on how one answers the question whether it is possible to be neurotic and authentic at the same time? If the answer is "no" then there is no significant difference between authenticity and organismic self-regulation. Authenticity in this case means being transparent with respect to one's own desires/needs. If, on the other hand, the answer is "yes" then they are quite the same. Authenticity in this case means to be transparent with respect to one's own neurosis. Nevertheless, the concepts are closely related. Both are concerned with our fidelity to what is truly our own and they both allude to some kind of truthful core that is in some more "us" than we ourselves are. Or maybe one should say *less* us, because it is ourselves minus our self-delusion and inhibitions.

12 Žižek (2013, 132) about Lacan's view: "The frustrating nature of our human existence, the very fact that our lives are forever out of joint, marked by a traumatic imbalance, is what propels us towards permanent creativity."

13 As Bloom puts it: "Any interruption in contactful reading became the center of attention. No question was trivial. Our reading was a psycho-dramatic exercise in hermeneutics" (Bloom, 2003).

14 Erving Polster on Fritz Perls's working style: "I never knew a magician and now I know what magicians can do" (Wysong & Rosenfeld, 1988, 55).

15 Those with most page occurrences in (Perls et al., 1994) and those with most sub-entries in (Polster & Polster, 1974). The difference in the method is due to the different logical structures of the indexes.

16 This is a reference to the gestalt community founded by Fritz Perls in 1969 at Lake Cowichan on Vancouver Island, Canada.

Bibliography

Aylward, J. (2014). Gestalt therapy and the dawn of postmodernism: A creative zeitgeist. In Bloom, D. & O'Neill, B. (Eds.), *The New York Institute for gestalt therapy in the 21st century: An anthology of published writings since 2000* (pp. 393–414). Ravenwood Press.

Bloom, D. (2003). We are all the New York Institute for gestalt therapy: Welcome to our fiftieth anniversary conference. In *gestalt alive!* New York Institute for Gestalt Therapy.

Bloom, D. (2019). Interviewed on March 6, 2019.

Bocian, B. (2010). *Fritz Perls in Berlin 1893–1933: Expressionism - Psychoanalysis - Judaism.* EHP - Edition Humanistische Psychologie.

Doubrawa, A., & Doubrawa, E. (Eds.). (2005). *Meine Wildnis ist die Seele des Anderen.* Peter Hammer Verlag.

Feder, B. (2015). *Origins of gestalt therapy.* Retrieved from https://youtu.be/ NZSEuN7QrTs

Frank, R. (2019). Interviewed on March 7, 2019.

Goodman, P. (1991). *Nature heals: Psychological essays of Paul Goodman.* Gestalt Journal Press.

Goodman, P. (2012). *Growing up absurd: Problems of youth in the organized society.* New York Review Books.

Greenberg, E. (2019). Interviewed on March 6, 2019.

Klepner, P. (2019). Interviewed on March 8, 2019.

Orwell, G. (1946). Politics and the English language. *Horizon,* 13(76), 252–265.

Perls, F. (1992). *Ego, hunger and aggression.* The Gestalt Journal Press, Inc.

Perls, F., Federline, R. F., & Goodman, P. (1994). *Gestalt therapy: Excitement and growth in the human personality.* The Gestalt Journal Press, Inc.

Polster, E. (2019). Interviewed on March 11, 2019.

Polster, E., & Polster, M. (1974). *Gestalt therapy integrated.* Brunner/Mazel Publishers.

Stier, T. (2009). *Here now next: Paul Goodman and the origins of gestalt therapy.* Routledge.

Weaver, J. (2019). *Creating gestalt therapy with Isadore From.* Retrieved from https:// vimeo.com/130464387

Wysong, J., & Rosenfeld, E. (1988). *An oral history of gestalt therapy.* Gestalt Journal Press.

Zevy, L. (2019). Interviewed on April 5, 2019.

Žižek, S. (2013). *Less than nothing: Hegel and the shadow of dialectical materialism.* Verso.

Chapter 2

The NYIGT and LGBT+ Community

The New York Institute for Gestalt Therapy was from its start known for its open-minded attitude toward the lesbian, gay, and bisexual community. In this chapter, I take a close look at this aspect of the institute's communal life. I sketch out the historical developments and provide a discussion of gestalt therapy theory connected to these phenomena. Additionally, I describe Identity House, which is an organization that grew out of the LGBT+ rights movement in the 1970s; it was founded by the institute members and was built on gestalt therapy principles.

Formation of a Community

It is a prime example of the progressiveness and social and political engagement of the New York Institute that it was the first psychological organization in the USA to consider homosexuality not as a pathological phenomenon but as a normal expression of the diversity of sexuality (Feder, 2015). For comparison, the American Psychological Association removed homosexuality from its diagnostic manual in 1973, that is, more than 20 years later (Genke, 1998). And it took even longer for the World Health Organization, which effectively removed homosexuality from its ICD manual in its tenth version in 1992 (Drescher, 2015; Mendelson, 2004).

> From the beginning gestalt therapy has always treated sexuality as an organic creative process that was often interrupted by the constraints and forces of societal definitions and repression. In keeping with this philosophy homosexuality by and large, was considered as just another form of sexual experience. Although there was little focus on understanding developmental process, therapy, particularly by the lesbian and gay practitioners who flocked to join this welcoming community, modeled new relational and environmental possibilities for deeply wounded, fearful clients.
>
> (Zevy, 2014, 335)

DOI: 10.4324/9781003296539-3

Thanks to gestalt therapy, there was at last a community of therapists who found astonishingly clear words to express the equality of sexual variations without any pathologizing connotations. In order to appreciate what this open-minded, truly humanistic, and radical standpoint meant, we have to consider the social and political context. So let us be reminded that the institute was founded in 1951 when the general atmosphere in society with regard to homosexuality was very oppressive:

> We should remember the squeamish, guilty, punishing attitude toward sexuality common not only in polite society, the conventional middle class, or the blue-collar masses, but almost as widespread among doctors, clinical psychologists, and psychoanalysts of just a generation ago. This attitude was all the more rigid and unyielding in the fifties simply because the repression was breaking down at last, and we were on the verge of sexual revolution of the sixties, whose reverberations are still echoing today.
>
> (Stoehr, 2009, 190)

One more excerpt from Here, Now, Next illustrates the uniqueness of gestalt therapy at that time:

> Aside from a few practitioners who followed their own lights, the only therapists of the postwar boom in psychotherapy who took actual sexual misery and its treatment seriously were the Reichians and the gestalt therapists. [...] But even the Reichians were notoriously homophobic. A friend of Goodman's who practiced as a children's therapist [...] went through a complete therapy with Reich himself without ever daring to reveal that he was homosexual! In contrast, a number of gestalt therapists were either bisexual, like Goodman, or homosexual, but whether they were or not, patients in gestalt treatment never had to be in the closet.
>
> (Stoehr, 2009, 191)

Or consider this account describing Laura Perls's erudite and progressive point of view.

> Bi-sexual Beat poet Harold Norse joined one of Laura's early groups consisting of lesbians and gay men and remembered her commenting on the term "homosexuality": 'It's inconvenient because of social prejudice, but I see nothing inherently wrong with it. Once a pleasure principle is established in sex, it can be more harmful to change it than to accept it.' A comment to which Norse responded: 'How civilized she is!'
>
> (Aylward, 2012, 124)

Because of its open-minded attitude, the institute became an attractive alternative for gay and lesbian psychologists, psychiatrists, psychotherapists, etc. who were otherwise confronted by the pathologizing attitude of their institutions. They gathered at the New York Institute and created a community with strong cohesion and bonding. Coming out often meant a considerable disruption and sometimes even severance of contacts in the biological family and Zevy points out that the community at the institute was more than collegial and social but to a large extent it became even more important than the family of origin (Zevy, 2019).

When I asked Zevy whether she could imagine the institute without this community, she answered with a resolute No! and added:

ZEVY: The beauty of being gay is that you are thrown into a highly creative environment, where you have to move away from all the traditional heterosexist models to create families and communities that work for you (Zevy, 2019).

Lazarin answered the same question in the typical laconic way of his that without the gays, the institute would not be so much fun (Lazarin, 2019b). And in Paul Goodman's words: "In my own case, however, being a [bisexual] seems to inspire me to want a more elementary humanity, wilder, less structured, more variegated, and where people pay attention to one another" (Goodman, 1991, 219).

Paul Goodman's Influence

It is mostly thanks to Paul Goodman that the institute developed this liberal and progressive attitude at the very beginning. His unapologetic openness with respect to his bisexuality is a well-known fact today, but more importantly, it was notorious then. Goodman's sexuality was a public affair and it is easy to imagine that he embodied the much yearned for freedom for those who otherwise felt confined and constricted by the repressive and homophobic conservative society and its conventional authorities. Goodman moved in intellectual and artistic circles[1] and he brought a number of his friends from there, some of them also bisexual or homosexual, to the institute.

This is not a place to recount Goodman's life in detail but a couple of short anecdotes are useful to get a sense of his renegade, in-your-face sexuality. For example, in 1939, Goodman, who struggled financially for the better part of his life, lost his teaching position at the university of Chicago because he refused to keep his cruising off the campus, and shortly after he got fired from another much needed job at a boarding school—for seducing his students. Goodman's behavior in the sexual arena was a source of concern even for the faculty of the experimental and liberal Black Mountain College, where he got a limited tenure for a summer session in 1950, and once again, he was thrown off the campus (Aylward, 2012, 101).

It was not only his behavior that raised some eyebrows but also the fact that he would not refrain from talking about it in public. As a therapist, he stayed true to his view of psychotherapy as an essentially practical discipline also in sexual matters:

> There were evenings, for example, when someone complained of a lack of sexual companionship, and Goodman would set about finding a solution in the room, if not one of the group then a date with some outside acquaintance. He turned to one person after another and asked each, What are you doing on Monday, on Tuesday, and so forth, and set up appointments for a whole week. There! See, that's not so hard, is it? he said.
>
> (Stoehr, 2009, 188)

It would be a mistake to ascribe Goodman's openness with which he demonstrated his sexuality only to some quirky aspects of his personality. His behavior was also a reflection and integral part of his political views and activism. For Goodman there was no real political freedom without sexual liberation. In this short quote, he links political change to the sexual liberation of adolescents and children:

> We must allow, and encourage, the sexual satisfaction of the young, both adolescent and small children, in order to free them from anxious submissiveness to authority. [...] This is essential in order to prevent the patterns of coercion and authority from re-emerging no matter what the political change has been.
>
> (Goodman, 2011, 43)

On a somewhat lighter note, Goodman lists his sexual advances, links them to his politics, and even gives a practical advice:

> In my observation and experience, queer life has some remarkable political values. It can be profoundly democratizing, throwing together every class and group more than heterosexuality does. Its promiscuity can be a beautiful thing (but be prudent about V.D.)
>
> I have cruised rich, poor, middle class, and petit bourgeois; black, white, yellow, and brown; scholars, jocks, Gentlemanly C's, and dropouts; farmers, seamen, railroad men, heavy industry, light manufacturing, communications, business, and finance; civilians, soldiers and sailors,

and once or twice cops. [...] There is a kind of political meaning, I guess, in the fact that there are so many types of attractive human beings; but what is more significant is that the many functions in which I am professionally and economically engaged are not altogether cut and dried but retain a certain animation and sensuality.

(Goodman, 1991, 219)

That it was Paul Goodman and not Laura Perls nor Fritz Perls who brought this view into gestalt therapy seems to be beyond doubt. In 1946, in a personal letter to a young man named Alex, who was concerned about his homosexuality, Laura Perls still carries a pathologizing view. She considers homosexuality as a half-dummy—referencing her theory of dummy-complex from *Ego, Hunger and Aggression*—positioned between fetishism (the complete dummy representing a contact with a lifeless object) and heterosexuality (the "proper" object of sexuality where one contacts a difference):

> What you have to realize is that in homosexuality you avoid the contact with something that is essentially different from you [...] That half-contact and homosexuality is one and the same thing.
>
> (Amendt-Lyon, 2016, 25)

If only Alex was able to properly experience difference, his homosexuality would be a "passing phase." While Laura Perls seemed to have softened or revised her point of view over time, probably thanks to the influence of Goodman and the community at the institute, Fritz Perls, who was not around the institute for long enough, did not. Some 15 years after the publication of *Gestalt Therapy*, Fritz Perls was still thinking in terms of cure and thus reiterated the prevalent medical and pathologizing standpoint:

> Now, for instance, in sex, the end-gain is the orgasm. The means-whereby can be a hundred different possibilities and as a matter of fact, the recognition of this by Medard Boss, the Swiss psychiatrist, is how he cured homosexuality. By having the patient fully accept homosexuality as one of the means to get to the organismic satisfaction, the end-gain, in this case the orgasm, he then had the possibility of changing the means-whereby.
>
> (Perls, 1975, 23)

This excerpt comes from *Gestalt Therapy Verbatim* which first appeared in 1969 and presents transcripts from Perls's Esalen workshops.

Goodman's spirit left a lasting imprint on the institute which keeps the flame of social activism burning to this day. All three founders were engaged politically, but Goodman maybe more than the others. After all, he earned his fame neither as an artist nor as a therapist but as a social critic when he published his book *Growing Up Absurd* (Goodman, 2012). Laura and Fritz Perls were politically active during their Germany times in Berlin (Bocian, 1998) but once they were in New York their direct public political engagement subsided. For Laura her political work moved to the therapy session[2] and Fritz concentrated on promoting gestalt therapy in other parts of the USA.

Identity House

In the 1970s in New York, an organization called Identity House was established. Its aim was to provide peer counseling services for the lesbian, gay, and bisexual community which at that time was experiencing what one might call a collective coming out. The famous Stonewall uprising in 1969 marks an important turning point in the emancipatory efforts of the LGBT+ community and Identity House was one among the many outcomes of that activism.

The story of Identity House is closely related to the story of the New York Institute and one cannot be told in its entirety without mentioning the other. Both organizations were built upon gestalt principles and there was a significant flow of people between the two. Two of the senior figures and influential trainers from the institute, Patrick Kelley and Karen Humphrey, were co-founders of Identity House and considerably shaped its functioning. Especially Kelley, who "supplied the necessary prophetic vision" for the project (Genke, 1998, 6). Many of the current Institute members got acquainted with gestalt therapy informally at Identity House and later joined the institute to start their training. And there are also those who learned about Identity House at the institute and started working there as counselors to gain practical experiences and apply what they learned in their training.

For my purpose of pursuing the goal of understanding the interplay of gestalt therapy theory and the community at the New York Institute, Identity House offers an ideal object of observation. For several reasons: it is based in New York, it brought together people from the margins (LGBT+ community in particular), it understands itself as a gestalt experiment, and self-reflectively applies gestalt therapy theory on itself. All of these facets are also part of the history of the New York Institute. At the same time, there are differences between the two organizations that allow for meaningful comparisons. First, Identity House was established 20 years after the institute by what one might call the second generation of gestalt therapists. Second, Identity House had a defined goal of providing services to people from outside of its organization, whereas the institute's purpose was to create teaching and learning community for its own members. Third, Identity House managed to create a non-hierarchical, membership-run and consensus-based organization right from the start, whereas it took the institute almost 40 years to arrive at that kind of functioning.

Identity House was formed in 1971 in New York by a group of lesbian and gay mental health professionals and laypersons. This group comprised people mainly with a background in existential, experiential, and humanistic therapies (e.g., Rogerian therapy, gestalt therapy, psychodrama, primal scream, and others), which at that time were burgeoning and gaining in attractiveness, partly as a reaction to the rigidity of psychoanalysis (Zevy, 2019).

The group had a radical idea: "They were determined to demonstrate that the so-called [homosexual] pathology was really societal, and it was therefore society's obligation to adjust, not gay individuals" (Genke, 1998, 6). This attitude comes directly from the way gestalt therapy theory was understood and lived at the New York Institute. Patrick Kelley (1980, 220), the person who provided the chief theoretical conception of Identity House put it like this:

> The gestalt concept that perhaps it is not necessarily the individual's task to adjust to society is clearly at odds with the conventional medical model. We gestalt therapists, in fact, hold that at times it is society's task to adjust to the individual.

Based on this principle, people are supported to make the next necessary steps derived from their individual needs without trying to impose some kind of normative idea of health. Once the needs are identified (made aware) they are respected as legitimate and appropriate.

According to Zevy (2019), the whole philosophy around Identity House was designed by Patrick Kelly, Karen Humphrey, Richard Kitzler—all three of them members of the NYIGT—and other experiential therapists. Although Kitzler was not directly involved, he was a close friend of Kelley and, in fact, they both lived on 16th Street, where Identity House was situated. Lazarin recounts that it took some fighting to establish this organization on gestalt therapy principles:

> The first two years of Identity House were turbulent years. Some of the founders pushed for a traditional social service organization led by professionally degreed people supported by dedicated cadre of volunteers. Others led by Kelley conceived of an entity organized with less imposed structure and a horizontal governance. These two contending visions led to breakups and regroupings. Before Identity House began fully functioning in 1973, two other organizations formed along hierarchical lines more akin to existing social services.
>
> (Lazarin, 2019a, 284)

Once these battles were fought out, Identity House took on a shape that it keeps to a large extent until today. Everyone involved in the organization professionally is a member and therefore has a voice. The decision process is based on consensus where every member has an equal voice. There is a re-volving leadership that changes every two years and this allows people from the membership to experience what it is like being administrators.

With respect to the offered services the guiding principle is that what the organization does and what systems it creates emerges from the people in the organization and their needs. The very original purpose of the organization emerged from the wider community because there was a need that was not being met.

The organizational structure of Identity House is kept flexible. Although it started with peer counseling, there was no notion at the beginning what it would mean in the long run. Groups that focused on certain topic were created organically when a certain need emerged among the people who came in, such as a drop-in group or a group for gay people in heterosexual marriages.

The organization has a specific flow of experience that follows organically the professional and personal growth of an individual. It starts with some-body coming to the Identity House and becoming a peer counselor. They at-tend a 12 weeks long supervision group and when they have worked enough with a more experienced peer they get a consensus to work alone. Consensus in this case means that the supervision group decides as a whole—by talking about the strengths and weaknesses—that the individual can counsel alone. Then they become the more experienced peer. When they take a short-term counseling training and work sufficiently, they can become short-term counselors, which means that they can work with a particular client for eight weeks on a particular topic like coming out in family or at work or breaking up a relationship.

Even though gestalt therapy is not explicitly taught at Identity House, the organization embodies it to such a degree that many of those I interviewed said that they learned gestalt therapy at Identity House without knowing it was gestalt therapy. Only later, when they joined the institute, they started to learn the theoretical foundations of what they had already experienced first hand. This is still true today:

ZEVY: I do lots of supervision with younger twenty, thirty year olds, who are going to go into the mental health field. Some of whom will go into gestalt therapy, some of whom will go into psychoanalysis. But they will be influenced by what happens at Identity House, because Identity House is still based on gestalt therapy principles. Still the same ones and that are still going strong today (Zevy, 2019).

Theoretical Considerations

Several principles and ideas from gestalt therapy theory are connected to the openness of the institute toward the LGBT+ community and in this sec-tion I take a closer look at some of them.

Conceptualization of Homosexuality

I could find only two passing mentions of homosexuality in *Gestalt Therapy*. The first one is in the practical volume and it expresses a kind of dated psychoanalytic view which cannot be called progressive or considered supportive of the liberal and emancipating attitude at the institute:

> homosexual love can frequently be analyzed as a still earlier projection of a more primary self-love — which was a retroflection that one was punished for or "shamed out of."
>
> (Perls et al., 1994, 464)

I wonder whether Goodman, as the co-author and the editor of the book, agreed with this formulation. Did he consider his own homosexuality as a projection of self-love? The second mention is to be found, smuggled as it were, in a section called *Formation of Personality: Loyalty*. The pertinent paragraph is the second one in the quote below, but in order to appreciate the subtle ambiguity of that formulation, it is important to include also the preceding one:

> An Italian peasant immigrant, loyal to his childhood, often refuses to learn English, though his ignorance hampers his present life: it is that he was too quickly and thoroughly uprooted and too many of the old situations were unfinished. On the other hand, a German refugee from Hitler learns English in a few weeks and completely forgets German: he needs to blot out the past and speedily make a new life to fill the void.
>
> In therapy, the so-called "regressions" are aware loyalties, and it is pointless to deny or denigrate what the patient has really felt as his own; the task is to find out the unaware unfinished situations that are taking energy from the possibilities of the present. The classical instance is the impossibility of "changing" homosexuals who have once gotten important sexual satisfaction, especially since they have creatively overcome many social obstacles in order to get it. The method is clearly not to attack the homosexual adjustment, for that has been the result of self's integrative power, it is a proved felt contact and identification. The method must be to bring to light what the personality is unaware alienating, here the interest in the other sex, half the human beings in the world.
>
> (Perls et al., 1994, 203)

How are we to understand it? We can see the positive and affirmative attitude toward homosexuality. What especially stands out is the rejection of attempts to change a homosexual. We can appreciate the importance of this statement if we remind ourselves of the pathologizing view of psychiatry and the widespread attempts to "cure" homosexuals with diverse conversion therapies at that time. As Genke (1998, 5) puts it:

> The homosexual milieu was then rife with horror stories about damages inflicted by practitioners of the medical model. Shock treatment, aversion therapy, and institutionalization were treatments of choice for the many whose culturally-evoked guilt and shame drove them into the arms of the 'helping' professions where their 'condition' was branded pathological.

The authors then follow with another important statement highlighting the struggle of overcoming social obstacles in order to arrive at a desired sexual satisfaction. They recognize the struggle and in a way critique the repressive society. However, the affirmation goes only so far. First, we should notice that homosexuality is presented only in its aspect of sexual satisfaction; other aspects such as intimacy, love, and relationship are not explicitly considered. And second, the authors conceptualize homosexuality as a creative adjustment *alienating* the interest in the other sex.

We can see how the formulation leaves room for interpretation: yes, homosexuality is not a pathological deviation from heterosexuality but it is an alienation and an unfinished situation nonetheless. It follows that something could be done about it. Like the Italian peasant who may eventually learn English and the German refugee who can one day make peace with the past, so the homosexual can become aware of and integrate their interest in the other sex. The use of the terms "alienation" and "unfinished situation" suggests that the authors were not able to emancipate themselves fully from thinking in terms of pathology. However, they also achieve a surprising equalization of homosexuality and heterosexuality. According to the presented formula, heterosexuality must likewise be understood as a creative adjustment: in this case, alienating the same sex. It follows that the only alternative for a well-integrated personality, one which is able to flexibly explore both poles, is bisexuality.

The passage sends mixed signals and does not arrive at a simple acceptance and affirmation of homosexuality without a caveat. On one hand, it offers a clearly positive message: homosexuality is a result of the integrative powers of the self and it is pointless trying to change a homosexual. But on the other hand, this positive message comes with an addendum in the form of alienation: the homosexual person is unaware alienating their interest in half of the potential sexual partners. Moreover, gestalt therapy offers a method to "bring to light what the personality is unaware alienating." It may be important to point out at this moment that the term "alienation" in the context of a humanistic psychotherapeutic school does not bring with it the same kind of weight and consequences as the word pathology does in the medical context. Whereas alienation describes a situation in its existential aspect, pathology points to the necessity or desirability of cure.

That this conceptualization of homosexuality is somewhat problematic finds an indirect proof in the way Patrick Kelley quoted this section. He uses the quote in order to support his claim that the theory provided a view, which respected the individual's sexual identity. However, we can see that he chose a very specific segment and the omissions are in this case quite telling:

Historically, gestalt therapy has attracted a large number of gays. It is our contention that his phenomenon occurred because it respected the integrity of the individual's sexual identity. "In therapy, the so-called 'regressions' are aware loyalties and it is pointless to deny or denigrate what the patient has really felt as his own;... The classical instance is the impossibility of 'changing' homosexuals who have once gotten important sexual satisfaction, especially since they have creatively overcome many social obstacles in order to get it."

(Kelley, 1980, 220)

Kelley leaves out a sentence that suggests that homosexuality represents an unfinished situation. Furthermore, if he continued the quote for two more sentences, he would have to deal with the uncomfortable part that speaks of homosexual alienation and suggests a method for overcoming it. The support found in the theory would immediately appear less firm and definite.

Despite its limitations, the view of homosexuality presented in *Gestalt Therapy* was significantly progressive and predated the changes in the outlook among professionals and the general public by decades. As I mentioned earlier, it was not until 1973 that the American Psychological Association (APA) removed homosexuality from its diagnostic manual. The general view nowadays is that homosexuality is not a pathological development and in most cases does not involve a conscious choice; and until today there is no general scientific consensus on its etiology. The APA's brochure from 2008 called *Answers to Your Questions For a Better Understanding of Sexual Orientation & Homosexuality* gives the following recommendation for therapists whose clients are concerned with their sexual orientation:

Helpful responses of a therapist treating an individual who is troubled about her or his same sex attractions include helping that person actively cope with social prejudices against homosexuality, successfully resolve issues associated with and resulting from internal conflicts, and actively lead a happy and satisfying life.

(APA, 2008)

We can see that the APA now recommends what gestalt therapy suggested from the very beginning: that "the problem was never what gave pleasure or satisfaction, only what prevented it" (Stoehr, 2009, 191). Due to its focus on the contact boundary of the organism and its environment, gestalt therapy was in a good position to avoid trying to provide a theory of homosexuality (and thus explain it away) but rather explore the problems that stood in the way of achieving sexual satisfaction.

Supporting the Figure Formation

The previous section shows that gestalt therapy's explicit conceptualization of homosexuality is somewhat ambiguous and problematic. Although Kelley used it in order to back his claim that gestalt therapy was accepting of the integrity of homosexuality, he was forced, as we have seen, to leave some parts of the conceptualization out.

One the other hand, what can be seen on the example of Identity House and heard from the testimonies of my interview with Zevy and Lazarin, is that the major theoretical cornerstone behind the accepting attitude of gestalt therapy was something else. It seems to me that the chief supporting principle was a more fundamental and general one. It was the idea that a therapeutic (i.e. emancipatory) effect can be achieved simply by following the emerging experience of the client and supporting its formation by bringing more awareness into the process.

It is a genuinely gestalt therapy idea that the "healthiness" of experience is not measured against some kind of objective standard imposed from outside, but by evaluating the intrinsic aesthetic qualities of what currently emerges:

> The therapy, then, consists in analyzing the internal structure of the actual experience, with whatever degree of contact it has: not so much what is being experienced, remembered, done, said, etc., as how what is being remembered is remembered, or how what is said is said, with what facial expression, what tone of voice, what syntax, what posture, what affect, what omission, what regard or disregard of the other person, etc. By working on the unity and disunity of this structure of the experience here and now, it is possible to remake the dynamic relations of the figure and ground until the contact is heightened, the awareness brightened and the behavior energized. Most important of all, *the achievement of a strong gestalt is itself the cure, for the figure of contact is not a sign of, but is itself the creative integration of experience.*
>
> (Perls et al., 1994, 8)

If what emerges is bright and strong and leads to satisfaction, it creates a good and closed gestalt and the organism can move on. A continuous and flexible figure formation is then considered to be a good functioning of the organism, which is the goal of therapy. In this process, there is no need for an external expert who knows what is healthy and what is pathological. Anyone sufficiently involved and interested is capable of describing and evaluating his or her own experience using this phenomenological method. The therapist does not have a final word on the meaning of the experience or how to interpret it. Their role is to provide just another perspective and an expertise in bringing more awareness into the experience (e.g. by commenting on the process, suggesting an experiment, sharing).

This process challenges a person to become aware of their needs, to take responsibility for them and pursue their fulfillment through a good contact with the environment. This principle can be applied to individuals as well as groups. Identity House provided examples of both. As individuals, people were supported and encouraged to seek the kind of love relationships they needed and desired. On the organizational level, Identity House was conceived such that emerging needs of the members could be identified and incorporated into its own structure and functioning.

Notes

1 Such as Living Theater, an avant-garde theater group for which Goodman also wrote a couple of plays.
2 "Ich denke, wenn man Menschen dabei unterstützt, authentischer zu werden—in Gesellschaften, die mehr oder weniger autoritär oder autoritätsorientiert sind, ist das immer politische Arbeit, in der Therapie, in der Erziehung, in der Sozialarbeit" (Doubrawa & Doubrawa, 2005, 119).

Bibliography

Amendt-Lyon, N. (2016). *Timeless experience: Laura Perls' unpublished notebooks and literary texts 1946–1985.* Cambridge Scholars Publishing.

APA. (2008). *Answers to your questions for a better understanding of sexual orientation and homosexuality.* American Psychological Association. Retrieved from https://www.apa.org/topics/lgbt/orientation

Aylward, J. (2012). *Gestalt therapy and the American experience.* Ravenwood Press.

Bocian, B. (1998). *Gestalt therapy and psychoanalysis: Toward a better understanding of a figure-ground relationship.* Gestalt Review, 2(3), 232–252.

Doubrawa, A., & Doubrawa, E. (Eds.). (2005). *Meine Wildnis ist die Seele des Anderen.* Peter Hammer Verlag.

Drescher, J. (2015). Out of DSM: Depathologizing homosexuality. *Behavioral sciences* (Basel, Switzerland), 5(4), 565–575.

Feder, B. (2015). *Origins of gestalt therapy.* Retrieved from https://youtu.be/NZSEuN7QrTs

Genke, J. (1998). *Identity House: The story of the growth and development of an alternative organization for lesbian, gay and bisexual adults.* Not published.

Goodman, P. (1991). *Nature heals: psychological essays of Paul Goodman.* Edited by T. Stoehr. Gestalt Journal Press.

Goodman, P. (2011). *The Paul Goodman reader.* Edited by T. Stoehr. PM Press.

Goodman, P. (2012). *Growing up absurd: Problems of youth in the organized society.* New York Review Books.

Kelley, P. (1980). Identity House: A gestalt experiment for gays. In B. Feder & R. Ronall (Eds.), *Beyond the hot seat: gestalt approaches to group* (pp. 219–228). Brunnel/Mazel.

Lazarin, B. (2019a). Identity House and a gestalt experiment revisited. *Gestalt Review*, 23(3), 282–292.

Lazarin, B. (2019b). Interviewed on March 8, 2019.

Mendelson, G. (2004). Homosexuality and psychiatric nosology. *The Australian and New Zealand Journal of Psychiatry*, 37(6), 678–683.

Perls, F. (1975). *Gestalt therapy verbatim*. Bantam Books.

Perls, F., Hefferline, R. F., & Goodman, P. (1994). *Gestalt therapy: Excitement and growth in the human personality*. The Gestalt Journal Press, Inc.

Stoehr, T. (2009). *Here now next: Paul Goodman and the origins of gestalt therapy*. Routledge.

Zevy, L. (2014). Lesbian Tomboys and "Evolutionary Butch". In Bloom, D. & O'Neill, B. (Eds.), *The New York Institute for gestalt therapy in the 21st century: An anthology of published writings since 2000* (pp. 335–350). Ravenwood Press.

Zevy, L. (2019). Interviewed on April 5, 2019.

Chapter 3

Democratization of the Institute

When the New York Institute for Gestalt Therapy (NYIGT) was formed, it was quite different from other institutes. The Institute's functioning and structure

> was widely influenced by Paul Goodman, who was an anarchist, and although it had certain amount of structure in order to qualify for non-profit status in the state of New York as an educational organization [...] the training was strictly in groups and there were no courses given, there were no classes, no requirements, no papers and no certificate of completion.
>
> (Feder, 2015)

The initial formal structure of the institute was such that Laura Perls was the "President in Perpetuity" but that role was to a great degree symbolic and did not entail much of the administrative work. The burden of running the institute was shouldered by the Vice President, the Treasurer, and the Secretary. There was a small group of important members called the Council of Fellows (Laura Perls, Isadore From, Richard Kitzler, Patrick Kelly, Karen Humphrey, to name a few) who were the sole holders of the decision power in the institute. They governed in an autocratic fashion: "they held meetings in secret" (Feder, 2015), and decisions were made without consulting the members. This is how Dan Bloom described the institute's structure in the 1980s:

BLOOM: The structure was that the Fellows were making decisions for the institute and the Associates were running it. The Associates were doing the work but did not have any say in what was being done. At the same time, the Fellows were getting older and uninterested. That continued over the 1980s. All of the warmth and affiliation at the institute, basically, was happening among the Associates who were meeting among themselves, more or less (Bloom, 2019).

DOI: 10.4324/9781003296539-4

Three categories of membership existed: Associates, Full Members, and Fellows. Anyone who registered and paid their dues could become an Associate. However, the process of becoming a Full Member—which meant that the member had a solid expertise in Gestalt Therapy and was eligible for referrals—was fully and opaquely in the hands of the Fellows. Bud Feder referred to the process of selecting Full Members pointedly as "anointing" (Feder, 2015). Recall also Greenberg's story of her first meeting at the institute (quoted in Chapter 1) where she relates how now and then people would stand up and ask *How does one become a full member?* and never get a straight answer. Having support from one of the senior figures was one way:

GREENBERG: I was married to Ed Rosenfeld, who introduced me to gestalt therapy. [...] I thought I'd better give it some strategic thought: Ed was very liked by Isadore From and so I decided to study with Isadore. Because, all these people, you had to beg them to study with them. Isadore would turn people away. I watched him being very nasty to people, turning them away. But I wasn't going to be turned away because I came through the Ed-door. [...] After three years [of studying with Isadore], I said "Well, I think I have enough for now"—which he was all surprised about; I guess people did not say that to him that often—"Would you recommend me for membership?". He was shocked, but he got over his shock—apparently this wasn't something anyone did—and he took a moment and said "Yes, I'd recommend you for membership". [...] Politically, it turned out to be a very astute move because who is going to say to him that I do not know enough gestalt therapy? (Greenberg, 2019)

And to become a fellow was a similarly obscure process completely in the hands of the Fellows. Ironically, those who founded the institute were from the start focused on not creating a hierarchical and autocratic organization. In an interview from 1985, Elliott Shapiro recalls the discussions which preceded the formation of the institute:

I remember our talking about developing the group as a group and also as an institute. And there was always the train of thought, "Yes we ought to develop this as an institute but we have to be careful that nobody's in charge, nobody's authoritative, that we are all equals" [...] I think our concerns about authoritarianism and equality got in the way of the institute in many ways, but nevertheless I respect it very highly, and I respect the fact that they managed to keep things that way all through the years.

(Wysong & Rosenfeld, 1988, 81)

Although they aspired to create a non-authoritarian organization, they achieved that goal only for themselves and failed in the eyes of the later generation.

In the 1980s, the younger members of the institute were becoming more and more self-supported and started to question the functioning of the organization and the contentious atmosphere at the meetings. They were growing up, building self-confidence, and initiated a transformational process at the institute which at the end of the 1980s led to its major restructuring (Klepner, 2019).

New Focus on Groups

Until about 1980, the predominant way for gestalt therapists to work in a group setting involved using the so-called hot-seat method (Feder, 2013, 37). In the hot-seat format, a person who wants to work goes to sit in a designated "hot seat" (usually the chair next to the therapist); he or she then works with the therapist individually; the rest of the group are more or less witnesses or a kind of chorus that occasionally provides feedback. This way of working in a group, which is basically an individual therapy in front of an audience, is well known and became almost synonymous with gestalt therapy. The impressive demonstration videos by Fritz Perls, who used the hot-seat method almost exclusively, were probably the main reason for this method's fame/notoriousness. The hot-seat work intensifies the experience for the person who is doing the work, but it completely disregards group dynamics.

Even though Laura Perls did not use a designated chair, in essence, she, too, used the hot-seat method. A person who wanted to work stayed at their chair and Laura worked with them individually while the rest of the group functioned as the audience. Neither did she show any concern for the group dynamics: she did not pay attention to themes that appeared in the whole group nor it became a topic if someone was missing or dropped out. Feder and Greenberg relate two similar incidents that illustrate this point. They happened on two different occasions in groups led by Laura:

> Ruth Ronall and I were in Laura's group for a year and a half [...] and during that time we developed a major dissatisfaction with one aspect of her way of working, which was to completely ignore group dynamics. If people had a relationship outside of the group that everybody knew about there will be no discussion, if somebody disappeared and never came back it would not be mentioned. One time [...] she brought in a guest without asking us, a guy from Israel who stayed for two sessions, monopolized the time and then disappeared.
>
> (Feder, 2015)

In Greenberg's case, Laura invited six people from Germany to join her training group on its first meeting. Greenberg recalls how she was unexpectedly attacked by one of the German women who felt ignored by her. When Greenberg, who was pregnant at that time and without an appetite for a conflict, suggested to work on the issue again in a week at the next group meeting, she was very surprised to learn that the guests came only for one session.

GREENBERG: I thought this is very badly run! Because Laura did not offer me any support or comment on what was going on. She did not say a word so this woman felt permission to engage in that way. I said 'Well, very New York Institute!' You know, I don't get an opportunity to work with her, she gets to dump, so what am I learning from this? Do I want to continue in this group?

When I followed up and asked Greenberg what it was that she actually learned from it, she replied:

I learned that sometimes when I'm going for what is bright and shiny to me — very gestalt — that there's somebody sitting in the corner who's not bright and shiny, who's feeling left out.

(Greenberg, 2019)

Bud Feder recounts how his training group led by Laura Perls transformed into a group run by all its members. Feder joined the group for training but in the second year Laura became seriously ill and had to undergo surgery after which she was recovering at her daughter Renate's house and could not work for about three months. One of Laura's training groups disbanded; however, Feder's group kept on meeting. The members were experienced psychiatrists, psychotherapists, social workers, art therapists, etc. with backgrounds in different modalities (such as bioenergetics, transactional analysis, and Rogerian therapy). Every week they would meet at the office of one of the group members and the host would lead the group in his or her modality. The experience was so satisfying that when Laura was fit enough to work and wanted to go back to lead the group again, the members did not want that and decided that they would instead invite her to join their group not as a leader but as a peer. Feder (2015) describes how anxious he was confronting Laura with the fact that her group was not hers anymore. To everyone's surprise, she agreed and the group continued for about five or six more years.

In 1980, a seminal book *Beyond the Hot Seat: Gestalt Approaches to Group* was published. It was edited by Bud Feder and his colleague from the training-group-turned-peer-group, Ruth Ronall. It is a collection of papers by 16 gestalt therapists,[1] from New York, Cleveland, and other institutes, describing their work with groups and new theoretical conceptualizations of group therapy from the gestalt perspective. As the title suggests, the book marks a departure from the "classical" hot-seat method. The authors present new approaches: they are looking at the group as a whole, consider its specific dynamics and shift the focus from intra-personal conflicts to interpersonal interactions. Feder (2013) gives a list of the main concerns of a group therapy based on group dynamics: leadership styles and their effects, membership, cohesion, pressures from other members, rules and norms, goals and tasks, phases in group development, the dynamics of power, and the effects of the group on the individual. For a detailed treatment of these topics, see for example, Cartwright and Zander (1968).

One may consider this change in focus (from the individual to the collective) as a kind of precursor to the democratizing changes at the institute. After all, the focus on group dynamics implies certain sensitivity toward all the members of a group. The departure from the hot-seat method is in itself a kind of democratization: what was once a chorus became a collective of equals interacting with each other, each one having an individual voice. The standing of the leader changes as well: from a kind of "director" in the spotlight of the individual work, she or he moves more into the background and becomes a group facilitator (Feder, 2013). It seems natural to come up with the hypothesis—formulated also by Zevy (Zevy, 2003, 72)—that when people started to look at therapeutic groups this way that they would use the same option to evaluate the situation at the institute and demand changes. This hypothesis obtains its indirect confirmation in words of Dan Bloom and Perry Klepner:

BLOOM: The shifting of the notion of gestalt therapy from figure of people having discussion to one in which the figure was seen as also in an organizational ground and the organizational ground needed to be paid attention to. Which is to say: The Associates, the Members… we need to take time to include everyone. That shifted in the 1980s. That is the time also when gestalt therapy began to be less figure-bound and to be much more concerned with figure-ground relationship and with what is really as plain as the nose on your face: the group process (Bloom, 2019).

Klepner talks about the culture the institute entered in the 1990s when the democratizing changes were already in place. In the following quote, he mentions Carl Hodges who was one of the persons who had spearheaded the changes.

KLEPNER: During the 1990s we were into a kind of new culture. Carl Hodges was the first President and he is always thinking in terms of field, field dynamics, and what is happening in the group. That is a very democratizing place to come to in a group: always searching the group for the forming figure and what is its meaning for us in a self-actualizing way (Klepner, 2019).

The new focus on groups, in the course of which the institute developed its own interpersonal, relational, and interactive approach (Bloom, 2019), culminated on December 7, 1991 when a conference on gestalt group therapy, organized by the institute, took place. It was also at this conference that the concept of *process groups* (Klepner, 2011) was implemented for the first time. The idea was originally developed by Carl Hodges and Richard Kitzler, and it quickly took roots and, nowadays, process groups are part and parcel of many gestalt conferences around the world.

Preparation

It is 1988 and every fellow has been Vice President, Treasurer, or Secretary at this point. The Fellows are worn out being autocratic (Feder, 2015) and are not rejuvenating (Klepner, 2019). They therefore decide that one of the Full Members should be the new Vice President. They ask Bud Feder but he refuses to do it because he does not want to be part of an autocratic governance. Then, they ask Carl Hodges and he, too, rejects the offer. Everyone they ask refuses, and the institute arrives at an important point, a crisis (Feder, 2015).

According to Klepner, it was to Carl Hodges' credit that the members refused to become part of the board and questioned the existing structure of the governance instead. They formed a group, which then formally became the Interim Executive Committee, where they pondered what kind of institute they wanted. This group was meeting from 1989 till 1990 and, in the course of the two years, they were rewriting the constitution of the organization in order to turn it into a democratic instead of an autocratic one.

Perry Klepner provided me with a battery of documents pertaining to these changes. These documents are an assortment of reports from meetings and letters to membership. They span a period of time from March 1988 to October 1992. They capture these transformational times of the New York Institute. Not only that they offer a close-up view of the processes, meetings, struggles, efforts, and development of ideas, they also display the way it was all talked about. The language is very "gestalt" and it supports the observation that throughout its history, the institute not only actively participated in the development of a new theory, but more importantly applied this theory to its own functioning and to its own self-reflections. In other words, the structure, the functioning, and the self-consciousness of the institute is inseparable from the theory and vice versa. For example, in the summary of a business meeting from March 1988, we can read:

> At the latest meeting, we focussed on the issue of the norms and values which govern our interactions at the institute meetings. We moved toward a consensus on the need for aggression which is issue and learning centered rather than power and dominance centered. We agreed there had been a change in the functional leadership. The Council of Fellows

were perceived to have become a fixed gestalt no longer serving a purpose. We wish next to find ways to address the issues of organization, management, and structures of the institute (i.e. the brochure, phone, etc.)

This short summary is teeming with references and several important points can be discerned. The language of norms and values points toward the application of group-dynamics theory and also toward the growing dissatisfaction among members about the aggressive and contentious atmosphere at the meetings. Aggression was discussed as well and not only as something negative, something to get rid of. Its central role in the theory of gestalt therapy and in the functioning of the institute was recognized as vital. Aggression, according to this short summary, was, therefore, not to be abandoned but somehow transformed: it should not serve the purpose of power and dominance but be directed at the understanding of the issues at hand.

The summary offers a succinct analysis of the institute's situation—expressed in gestalt terms. The Council of Fellows is diagnosed as a fixed gestalt which no longer serves its original purpose. The functional leadership, as the summary points out, has shifted. Toward what? Bud Feder's account above corroborates the answer to this question: whereas the Fellows retained the power to make decisions, the members did the hard work. A fixed gestalt is something that originally was a spontaneous reaction to a situation, a creative solution to some problem, that however became habitual, out of awareness, and therefore fixed. As the field situation changes, the fixed gestalt may lose its functionality and the solution which it had provided may itself become a problem. In short, as the field conditions change any fixed gestalt can become dysfunctional and this summary identifies the Council of Fellows as such.

Besides the aforementioned points, the summary is one more example of how the institute self-reflectively applied gestalt theory and terminology to its own functioning. Two aspects are figural here: the "diagnosis" of a fixed gestalt and the ongoing recognition of aggression (in other words, the refusal to abandon aggression). In theory, it is the combination of awareness and the destructuring capacity of aggression that is needed for a fixed gestalt to be taken apart and thus make space for a new figure. The use of the word *consensus* also points toward the direction of democratization that the institute is about to take.

Seven months later, in October 1988, the Structure and Organization Committee created a document called a *Statement of Purpose* which defined the new contours of the institute. This document is worth quoting in full length:

We want a place/space to learn about Gestalt Therapy, a place where we could learn from and teach each other, debate and explore issues in Gestalt Therapy Theory, share our questions and exchange ideas. A place where we could pursue the development of Gestalt Therapy Theory and its application to new areas.

We want a place safe for experimentation, a place where it is safe to be 'creatively ignorant' and have the opportunity to learn. A place where one can find recognition along the journey toward becoming a fully trained and competent gestalt therapist.

We want an atmosphere, at meetings, in which members respect each other and each other's differences in experience, training and seniority. An atmosphere in which members could challenge and confront each other, and in which aggression is issue and learning centered, rather than power and dominance centered.

Such a "place" could not be rented or legislated, but could only be built — continuously created by the aggressing of its members. The responsibility for creating and maintaining such a place and atmosphere lies with each of us. The responsibility for meeting our learning needs must be exercised by each one of us.

We would like to believe that Gestalt Therapy is more than a psychotherapy, encompassing a way of looking at and being in the world. This is by no means a unanimous view, and we welcome our differences. We believe that our Institute can embody the principles of contact, figure/ground, and gestalt formation and destruction which we describe in our theory, and we would want a structure as flexible and open to contacting as possible. Indeed structure can thus emerge from the needs, interests, and excitements of our members and thereby be vital, fluid, graceful and vigorous.

We want an Institute that is not insular but ethnically, professionally, and intellectually diverse. We want an Institute that reaches out to the wider community with service, education, information — and contact.

(Klepner, 2020, 3)

As with the meeting's summary given above, this statement of purpose is eloquently deploying gestalt therapy terminology in order to draw contours of the future institute. The text is explicit about the intention that the institute should "embody the principles of contact, figure/ground and gestalt formation and destruction." We can observe here clearly how the theory is extended beyond the scope of therapy and applied to structuring and supporting a community. Also, as the NYIGT is itself a place for the development of the theory, we can speak here of self-reflective application of its own "produce": the theory, which is taught and developed at the institute, is applied to its own functioning and structuring. And by doing this, the institute in a way proves the point that the Statement of Purpose expresses as a belief: namely, that the gestalt therapy theory is more than a psychotherapy.

The Statement of Purpose is a strong call by the emancipated younger generation for a radical change. It is almost a manifesto, bold and self-confident, fortified by the gestalt therapy theory. After its publication, it was time for the Interim Executive Committee (IEC) and other involved members to get into the work of implementing their vision.

Execution

From October 1988 until December 1990, the institute was in transition. The minutes of the meetings and letters to membership report about the steps taken. There were a lot of practical questions which the committee had to address. Some of the questions were answered in a discussion and some by experimentation. The IEC laid out the general direction the institute should take: it should continue as a membership organization, where the power resides in the membership and where the structure is kept flexible, reaffirmed, or changed every year (Klepner, 2020, 5). There were many details that had to be figured out.

Selection of New Full Members

As I mentioned earlier, until 1991, there were Fellows, Full Members, and Associates, but there was no clear process as to how one becomes a Full Member or a Fellow. It was the task for the IEC to provide clarity. They had to decide what categories of membership would exist and how one becomes eligible for one membership category or the other. There were various proposals, ranging from just one membership category to four (Associates, Full, Fellows, and Trainers). The discussions converged on the variant with three categories, the same ones as the institute already had, only that the category of Fellows did not carry with it any formal power any more. It was a category reserved for distinguished members:

> These Fellows would — as a balance to our loose and fluid structure — provide a kind of continuity as the repositories of the institute's traditions, history, and values. The title would not be merely honorific. These heretofore Fellows would be senior, skilled and demonstrably expert. They would be able (required?) to teach formally or informally, and would be active as models in our meetings.
>
> (Klepner, 2020, 4)

This passage comes from the Committee's report of its February meeting in 1989. An indeed, in 2001, after three long years of discussions and consensus-finding, Dan Bloom, Perry Klepner, Lee Zevy, and Carl Hodges became Fellows; they are currently the only ones at the Institute holding this distinction. As to the question how one becomes a Full Member, the search for answers was not straightforward and in the end, it was answered in the spirit of gestalt therapy by way of experimentation. Initially, it was suggested that there be a Membership Committee which oversees the process of becoming a Full Member. But that raised a lot of new questions. The February report continues:

> How would the Committee's membership be selected? elected? appointed? etc. What would be its composition: a certain number of Fellows (as defined above) would obviously be useful, as would a certain number of Members who are Trainers. Should an Associate also be on the committee? Would he or she be able to "vote"? Would the Committee's decision be by vote? or by consensus? Could there be appeal of its decisions? How long would its members serve (staggered terms?)? What would be the consequences of their "judgments" in an egalitarian membership organization? How would someone be proposed to become a new "Member?" Would the Committee also propose new "Fellows?" Would the membership at large ratify (or conversely "veto") their decisions? These issues, though identified, were left far from settled. But it was agreed that this would be an extremely important Committee.

It took a year to resolve these questions and arrive at a solution. The report from the committee's January meeting in 1990 informs members that after a lively discussion it was decided that the process of selecting new Full Members would be tested in form of a "radical experiment" (Klepner, 2020, 11). The idea of a designated Membership Committee was abandoned in favor of a process in which the membership-as-a-whole goes through interviewing and selecting new Full Members. The experiment took place at the very next institute meeting and four new members had been selected: Cynthia Cook, Gayla Feinstein, Ruella Frank, and Eric Werthman.

In the course of the experiment, the process of selecting new members took on its final form and was codified in the January report:

> Potential members must each be sponsored and nominated by two members (Full members and/or Fellows), who are familiar with their work and person. The potential new member must be present, to speak about her or himself, and to answer questions from any of those present. This experiment puts a tremendous responsibility not on some elite committee, but on the sponsoring members who propose someone for membership, an on each individual member and associate who must make sure that the interview and follow-up discussion are handled contactfully with both aggression and support. This is the only way an authentic consensus, a strong gestalt, can emerge.

Peter Philippson, who was proposed for the full membership by Bud Feder, gives an account of his experience of the process:

PHILIPPSON: It's like a British gentlemen's club in that you have to be proposed by a couple of members, put your name forward and there is then a meeting of the New York institute to discuss full-membership proposals. Everybody who has proposed themselves as full members has to present themselves and what their background is and what they offer to the institute. The term that was used in those days was "with full aggression". They didn't want passengers. They wanted people who would come in and take a full part (Philippson, 2021).

As much as the democratization was also a movement against an intimidating atmosphere at the meetings, the concept of aggression was preserved in writing and practice and continued to shape the functioning of the community. Philippson continues:

PHILIPPSON: I went over to New York—this would be around 1997 or 1998—and of course [traveling from Manchester] it was much later for me, it was I think two o'clock in the morning British time, so it all has an air of unreality. But I managed to present with full aggression and then the assembled members discussed my request for full membership. There were probably about thirty, forty people. They could ask me any question they liked about anything and then they voted in front of me. I remember the night when I put myself forward. There were two other people who put themselves forward and it certainly wasn't an automatic thing. One of the other people was not accepted and the third one was accepted but with quite a lot of discussion and questioning. So, it felt like really quite an event, quite a rite of passage (Philippson, 2021).

Organizational Structure and Functioning

When it came to the decision how the institute should be organized administratively, the Interim Executive Committee seemed to have a clear picture early on. In a letter to membership from November 1989—halfway through the transition process—Carl Hodges writes:

Dear Member:
    At our October meeting I was asked to summarize our discussion of how the institute should be organized with respect to administrative functions, decision making and officers. While we did not reach a clear consensus on these matters, the following presents my impression of what was being proposed.
    Organizationally, the institute would have a President, a Secretary […], and a Treasurer. These positions would fulfill the requirements of our charter and administrative functions necessary to maintain the institute's day-to-day and other usual activities. For example: arrangements

for monthly meetings, correspondence with the membership, dues collection, signing legal documents, possibly but not necessarily chairing monthly meetings, chairing business meetings, etc.

Decisions on Institute policies, programs and procedures would be made by the institute's members and associate members by consensus of those present at meetings. This will be done after the membership have been given notice and information on issues by mail. Issues which require immediate attention may come up at the meeting and could be decided without pre-notification by mail.

In addition, Institute Committees — as is the case currently with the Interim Executive Committee and Conference Committee — would be organized to carry out specific tasks such as reviewing listings in Institute brochure, preparing a presentation program for the forthcoming year, outreach, publicity, etc., as decided upon by the membership. Participation on committees would be encouraged within the institute.

This design is proposed with the intent of fostering an organization that values volunteerism and a membership that is participating in the institute's activities and leadership.

The design outlined in Hodges' letter is the one that was also adopted, and to this day, the institute functions as envisioned here.

The Result

As a result of these efforts, the functioning of the New York Institute changed significantly. The restructuring took on the formal form on Wednesday, December 5, 1990 when Carl Hodges, Karen Humphrey, Gayla Feinstein, and Eric Schneider were elected as the institute's officers, the President, the Vice President, the Treasurer, and the Secretary, respectively. The institute became a membership-run organization where decisions are reached by consensus process and where the presidency is a revolving two-year term position. The process of becoming a Full Member was stated explicitly and became transparent. According to the gestalt principle of emerging figure, the institute's "needs" are catered for by volunteering members who organize themselves in various more or less temporary committees. This is an excerpt from a report of the first administrative meeting after the changes:

> Carl, Karen, Eric and [Gayla] met and decided such mundane things as putting the management of the phones back on a monthly rotating basis among the members, developing an active and an expanded mailing list, and how to pick up the mail. We also took time to consider what the role of "officers" might be, in an organization in which power is entrusted in the membership. It was our sense that the task of the officers will be to "secure" the grounds (space, time, money communication, etc.), so that

the process and experiment which we as an Institute have been engaged in, can continue.

We also shared our "visions" of what we wanted for the institute [...] We want to continue our Institute's emphasis on having solid theoretical base, and we would solicit presentations which look at Gestalt Therapy's roots and foundations, which elucidate concepts and issues in our theory, and which apply the theory to our new areas. We want to honor and embrace the different styles which have developed in doing Gestalt Therapy and to support members in developing their own styles.

[...] Finally, the officers realized that all future "administrative" meetings must be posted and open to the general membership. The next one will be on Friday, January 28, 1991 at 8:00 PM at [Gayla] Feinsteins' Manhattan office. All are welcome.

(Klepner, 2020, 18)

And what is it actually like to be a president in this newly democratized institute?

ZEVY: It's like herding cats! [Laughs] Everybody has their own way of doing things. Everybody has an opinion. Everybody has likes and dislikes and you can't get everybody together to handle things in one form. As President I wanted to get more organization into the running of things, so I came up with a plan that had to do with committees. To some extent it worked and to some extent I couldn't get certain committees together. Like the marketing-outreach committee, never really formed, governance committee, never really formed (Zevy, 2019).

An Institute Echoing the World's Events?

If we zoom out from New York and look at the world situation in around 1989 we can see that there were immense democratizing efforts happening almost all around the world: the Tiananmen Square protests in China, the revolutions in Eastern Europe, the beginning of dissolution of the Soviet Union, the first democratic presidential elections in Brazil in 30 years, and the first democratic general elections in Chile in 16 years. One is tempted to say that democratization was "in the air" and did not spare the New York Institute either. It is almost as if the institute functions as a kind of resonator for the social and political phenomena that are present in the wider field.

From the perspective of Kurt Lewin's field theory—which, when boiled down to its most rudimentary statement, says that any element of the field is continually influenced by the whole situation and its behavior is a function of this element and its environment—one may look at the democratizing changes at the institute as reverberations of the democratizing changes that were happening around the world.

Lewin's field theory is an integral part of the gestalt therapy theory from the very start (Yontef, 1999, 179)—implicitly via the concept of holism in *Ego, Hunger and Aggression* (Parlett, 1991) and explicitly referenced in *Gestalt Therapy*. In accordance with this theory, gestalt therapists are trained to look for and recognize manifestations of the larger field's phenomena in the process of the current contact situation, be it in individual therapy, in a group, organization, or some other setting.

Perls and Goodman remind us of caution when it comes to identifying the relevant wholes and warn us specifically against making the whole too encompassing, too far-reaching (Perls et al., 1994, 54, 59). So we should heed their request and be cautious. After all, considering the world situation as the co-determining whole may indeed be too much. Yet, not every element of a field is equally sensitive to the events outside and the history of the New York Institute seems to provide evidence that this particular group of people was acutely attuned to the wider social and political aspects of its environment. Consider, for example, its pioneering stance against pathologizing homosexuality, which made it a forerunner in that regard (Chapter 2), or the parallels between the feminist movement and the efforts of the institute's women caucus (Chapter 4). Or one last example: nowadays, according to Adam Weitz, the institute grapples internally with what he calls "us against them" polarization which pits the young against the old and which he considers reflective of the social situation in the USA (Weitz, 2019).

What in gestalt therapy theory could be inducing such sensibility toward the phenomena of the larger field? And is there something special in this regard about the NYIGT? First of all, if we subscribe to the point of view of Lewin's field theory, then it is simply an a priori fact that the elements manifest, in one way or the other, the situation of the whole. The situation directly co-determines the element's behavior. However, the question here is a more specific one. The aim is to inquire into the degree of sensibility and susceptibility of the New York group toward the larger field's phenomena. I have provided a part of the answer already: Lewin's theory is part and parcel of gestalt therapy's thinking and as such sensitizes its students toward its own manifestations. But there are also other aspects of the theory that may contribute to such sensitivity.

The subtitle of *Ego, Hunger and Aggression* was "A Revision of Freud's Theory and Method" but it turned out to be more than a revision: it foreboded a significant turn, shift, and departure, which was then completed in *Gestalt Therapy*. One of the important changes was that gestalt therapy turned away from the interpretation of the unconscious—in fact, unconscious played only a minor role in the new theory—and turned toward *phenomenological exploration of the contact situation*. It focused on the self which is understood to be a system of contacts that occur at the boundary of the organism and its environment. The self is said to be formed *of* the boundary rather than residing *at* it and so the boundary belongs neither exclusively to the organism nor just to the environment; it belongs to both. This shift in perspective implies a conception of a self, which emphasizes the dynamic give-and-take interaction of the organism with its environment. In a way, the environment is the primary concern for the organism (as the place where it can potentially fulfill its needs) and gestalt therapy aims at re-establishing functional interactions at the contact boundary. That includes keeping an eye on one's social, ecological, and political environment and to engage with it actively and aggressively.

Another aspect of gestalt therapy theory which seems to contribute to the individual or group sensitivity toward the phenomena of the larger field is the emphasis on experimentation and the importance of ongoing and flexible figure formation. The flexibility of figure formation, that is, the capability of an organism to react sensibly, creatively, and functionally to the possibly widest spectrum of situations, is seen as a mark of healthy functioning. In other words, a healthy organism, as it moves from one situation to another, and from one environment to another, is constantly changing. For an organization which purports to be built on gestalt therapy foundations and pursues healthy functioning, it is, therefore, required that it inspects its own dysfunctional fixed gestalts, avoid or destroy them, and keep evolving and changing. We can see it in the above quote from the meeting minutes where the Council of Fellows was explicitly identified as a "fixed gestalt no longer serving its purpose." Gestalt therapy's methodological approach to keep the figure formation flexible is basically experimentation, which in more detail means: increasing awareness for the given situation, deconstructing fixed meanings, and trying out new solutions.

The New York Institute is an organization which prioritizes change and growth, and so it lends itself to being influenced or even swayed by external forces and the phenomena of the larger field. Lewin's field theory, the concept of contact boundary, and the importance of an ongoing figure formation are foundational theoretical aspects that contribute to sensitization of an individual or a group for the phenomena of the larger field.

Note

1 Six of the 16 authors (Feder, Kelley, Kitzler, Laves, Rapp, and Ronal) were affiliated with the New York Institute.

Bibliography

Bloom, D. (2019). Interviewed on March 6, 2019.

Cartwright, D., & Zander, A. (1968). *Group dynamics: research and theory.* Harper and Row, Publishers.

Feder, B. (2013). Gestalt *group therapy: A practical guide.* Ravenwood Press.

Feder, B. (2015). *Origins of gestalt therapy.* Retrieved from https://youtu.be/NZSEuN7QrTs

Greenberg, E. (2019). Interviewed on March 6, 2019.

Klepner, P. (2011). Process groups—A gestalt therapy conferencing experiment and the AAGT 2010 biennial conference. In D. Bloom & P. Brownell (Eds.), *Continuity and change: gestalt therapy now, the10th biennial conference of the Association for the advancement of gestalt therapy* (pp. 44–62). Cambridge Scholars Publishing.

Klepner, P. (2019). Interviewed on March 8, 2019.

Klepner, P. (2020). Collection of the NYIGT's meeting reports and letters to membership. Not published.

Parlett, M. (1991): Reflections on field theory. *The British Gestalt Journal*, 1(2), 69–81.

Perls, F., Hefferline, R. F., & Goodman, P. (1994). *Gestalt therapy: Excitement and growth in the human personality*. The Gestalt Journal Press, Inc.

Philippson, P. (2021). Interviewed on June 15, 2021.

Weitz, A. (2019). Interviewed on April 27, 2019.

Wysong, J., & Rosenfeld, E. (1988). *An oral history of gestalt therapy*. The Gestalt Journal Press, Inc.

Yontef, G. M. (1999): *Awareness, Dialog,* Prozess. EHP - Verlag Andreas Kohlhage.

Zevy, L. (2003). Self of group. In *gestalt alive!* New York Institute for Gestalt Therapy.

Zevy, L. (2019). Interviewed on April 5, 2019.

Chapter 4

The Women's Caucus

The end of the 1980s was an important time in the history of the institute and its community. Besides the efforts for its democratization, there was another movement—organized by women—that had a significant impact on the institute's culture. The starting point was, on one hand, a growing dissatisfaction among women with the combative atmosphere at the monthly meetings and, on the other hand, their increased self-support and self-confidence. They organized into a caucus that successfully challenged the prevailing culture from a feminist standpoint.

New Voices at the Institute

The institute was not a boy's club where women would be excluded or men would have an overwhelming majority. After all, Laura was the figurehead and when we take a look at the video recording from the 1988 meeting (described in Chapter 1), we can see a more or less 50-50 distribution of men and women. The inquiry into the women's position at the institute was never a question of numbers. The feminist movement, which since the 1970s in the USA was going through its so-called second wave, provided a critical analysis of the age-old oppression of women. Feminist theories, such as The Dialectic of Sex (Firestone, 1972), were instrumental in understanding the social/power dynamics pertaining to sex and gender and the resulting inequality and oppression. Some women at the institute were active feminists, Gayla Feinstein and Lee Zevy for example. They had the language and perspective to recognize gender-specific patterns at the institute and they started to question the prevailing culture. Zevy reports:

ZEVY: The 1970s were burgeoning days of the women's movement. I was very involved in the women's movement and I was very involved in the gay rights movement. The book [*Gestalt Therapy* by Perls, Hefferline, and Goodman] was written from a men's perspective. He this, he that. At one point I raised the question at an institute meeting whether we should take a look at women's position in gestalt therapy and Laura

DOI: 10.4324/9781003296539-5

said, "There's no difference in gestalt therapy" and that ended that. There was no discussion beyond that.

In Laura's worldview, because there were women at the institute there was no difference. But when you have read the book and you have read the theory, there was a section in PHG about deflowering a virgin which to my way of thinking [Zevy laughs] was an obvious problem. And also, for the most part, the people who argued at the institute were men. The women sort of kept quiet and people who were new kept quiet.

My point of view was that there was not a lot of room for women who tended to be more cautious about saying certain things. Women who were just coming into their own in the seventies and needed a certain kind of support to come forward as did new members of the institute (Zevy, 2019).

Why did Laura not recognize the merit in what Zevy was pointing to? The answer to this question goes to the core of the issue the feminists at the institute were raising. In a letter published in the *British Gestalt Journal*, Daniel Rosenblatt (1994) remembered Laura and her position at the institute:

Laura was an unrepentant high-brow, or if you will, an intellectual snob, and I honored her for it. At the beginning of twentieth century when she was born, Nietzsche and Freud were the avant-garde in philosophy and psychology, and she was well versed in both. In our conversations she would casually quote Rilke or Aristotle, Heidegger, Husserl or Plato. She was unapologetic for her learning.

Her stance — which might today be considered a radical feminist stance — led her to associate with the most difficult and enlightened ideas of her time. Laura often said she had no trouble as a woman in intellectual circles — that she was considered 'one of the boys.' Feminists today might challenge her, but I think Laura meant she was accepted as an intellectual equal by the men. Yet she did not have to devalue her femininity or become asexual in order to achieve this position.

I disagree with Rosenblatt that what he describes can be considered a radical feminist stance. Given his account is accurate, Laura comes out of it as an emancipated and empowered woman but not as a feminist. To be considered "one of the boys," which sounds quite like a promotion to men's ranks, was never a feminist goal. Rather than joining a game where the rules benefit the men, a radical feminist aims at setting up a totally new game. The goal is not promotion but revolution. In Firestone's words (1972, 15), the aim of radical feminism is to:

overthrow the oldest, most rigid class/caste system in existence, the class system based on sex — a system consolidated over thousands of years, lending the archetypal male and female roles an undeserved legitimacy and seeming permanence.

Any uprooting of the inherent power imbalance would inevitably threaten men's position. But Rosenblatt's formulation—"she was accepted as an intellectual equal by the men"—shows that it was still the men who did the accepting and so the fact that Laura was a woman did not challenge the status quo. What Rosenblatt celebrates in his letter is Laura's personal emancipation, one which ultimately remained in the framework of the preexisting (i.e. patriarchal) order. But the institute's feminist were after a different thing: they questioned the very order and they wanted to create new field conditions where they could experience a feminine way of being without having to play the boys' game. To inquire into Gestalt Therapy as being written from a male perspective is to inquire into the implicit foundations upon which the text stands. The answer to that cannot happen in terms of personal emancipation within the limits of the pre-existing order as the question itself is already breaking through these limits.

The Creation of the Women's Caucus

The Women's Caucus came to existence as a reaction to what some women recognized as a male-dominated culture at the institute. Gayla Feinstein had observed that at the meetings, it had been mostly men speaking, engaging, and arguing with each other while the women had often stayed quiet. Feinstein recounted that although she had been already a member for about 12 years she was still relatively shy. But she was surprised and perplexed to see experienced and accomplished women therapists and trainers, whom she knew as eloquent and self-confident from the smaller groups, being silent during the large meetings. Puzzled by her observation, she spoke with other women, and they confirmed that they, too, found the style of the meetings discouraging. Motivated by these confirmations and having experiences from a feminist movement, Feinstein initiated the creation of the institute's Women's Caucus. This group of women would meet regularly for a couple of years. They investigated and explored the cultural biases and expectations that limited and inhibited their free expression. The situation for women at the institute was such that just the mere fact of the creation of the caucus seemed radical and scary:

GREENBERG: Despite Laura being involved [the institute] was very masculine. It was so masculine that the women one time got together, and I joined them in this, though I was not much of a joiner usually, and we did what felt incredibly radical at that time and scary because the New York Institute, I don't care what anyone tells you, is a scary place to me (Greenberg, 2019).

In their regular meetings, the women of the Women's Caucus managed to identify the mode of operation of a group in which they would feel comfortable, supported with a sense of connection to each other. Feinstein[1] describes the main insights like this:

FEINSTEIN: But what was most figural was the *how* of being together: allowing a slowed tempo, pausing, turning inward, connecting with breath, heart and earth, thus developing a fuller presence and deepening the connections with each other. We were able to listen to one another in a more open, attentive and receptive way. There was a cooperative, warm and kind engagement that felt comfortable, inclusive and supportive.

Their explorations bore fruits for the whole of the institute: in 1991, they presented their findings in the form of two gestalt experiments at the monthly large meetings and made a significant impact on the institute and changed its culture.

The Two Experiments

In 1991, the Women's Caucus organized two experiments which would mark an important shift at the institute. The experiments were an outcome of the monthly meetings that the Women's Caucus had held for the previous year and a half. As a result, the institute's culture changed to be more inclusive, more relational, less combative, and less contentious.

Both experiments were set up as a *fishbowl*, which is a way of structuring a group process such that the participants sit in two concentric circles. The group in the inner smaller circle engages in activity while the persons in the larger outer circle are observing. Occasionally, some participants from the outer circle join the inner circle or the other way round. The fishbowl is a general scheme of an experiment; however, when someone at the NYIGT talks about "the fishbowl experiment," they usually mean one of these two pivoting events from 1991 organized by the Women's Caucus and presented at the monthly meetings.

The two experiments were: (1) the women circle and (2) reading of PHG while substituting she for he, her for his, etc. The women challenged the culture, which they have seen as masculine, marked by one-upmanship, and different to how these women related to each other in their women-only meetings.

The two experiments are illustrative of the NYIGT's commitment to gestalt theory as the shaping force for the institute itself. Here, the experimental paradigm of gestalt therapy is applied to the ways of being of the community. The awareness that arises out of that process is not codified in a written resolution or a rule. Instead, the change is left to the process of self-regulation of the members and the community.

The Women Circle Experiment

The purpose of the women circle experiment was to present and make expe-
rienceable what a group where women felt comfortable looked and felt like.
Gayla Feinstein describes how it went:

FEINSTEIN: We formed a fishbowl. The women of the caucus sat in the center
of the larger circle. We stayed with and attended to our process—the
moment-to-moment experiencing and sharing. Then after about a half
an hour we asked for a male volunteer to join our circle. Eric volunteered and came into the fish bowl. The responses of the women varied:
some were welcoming and others recoiling as they moved their chairs
back. Awareness offered itself to us as we stayed present with our experience. Our pace and rhythm continued to invite and support a more
embodied relational engaging as we stayed with the process and our
experience of what it was like to have him join us. We did that for about
20 minutes and asked for another man to come in. We continued the
slower tempo allowing for a more alive and contactful meeting as we
rested in the rhythm of reciprocity. Then we invited another man in and
continued with our process.

From that point on the field really shifted at the institute. There was
space and support for women to add their voices and participate more
freely and fully. There was an intimacy and inclusiveness that enriched
the field leading to a more respectful, cooperative, and accepting way. It
was a really exciting time (Feinstein, 2019).

Lee Zevy corroborates Feinstein's account and relates how the inviting of
a man into the circle of women had an effect on her and Richard Kitzler:

ZEVY: At some point they invited a man in, who was Eric Werthman, and
the minute he came in, I pushed my chair back because he was six foot
something. That had a very profound effect on Richard because he saw
for the first time the relative differences in how men and women occupy
space. There was something about that that rang true for him, and the
way in which conversation shifted when Eric came into the group. At
that point, the institute started to shift to a different way of being. It
became less argumentative, it became less contentious and less competitive (Zevy, 2019).

Reading PHG with Feminine Pronouns

The other experiment which was part of the shift consisted of reading from
Gestalt Therapy (PHG) while substituting masculine pronouns with feminine ones. The experiment provided several experiential opportunities: The

men could experience what it is like to hear or read a text where the masculine is included only by assumption and excluded literally. For the women, it meant to experience a text that speaks directly to them and of them. Yet another opportunity was to uncover the unconscious (implicit, unspoken, forgotten, habitual, and so forth) assumptions behind this particular male-bound way of writing and thinking. In gestalt therapy terms, the experiment would bring awareness into the authors' and readers' confluence with the ever-present background of the societal norm reflected in the language usage. For Gayla Feinstein, the changing of "hims" to "hers" was a powerful experience:

FEINSTEIN: The experiment was so simple and yet, stunning. Living in a patriarchal culture we certainly were aware of the beliefs and biases imposed upon and assimilated into us often resulting in struggles to embody our sufficiency, worthiness and value. How do we find the divine within ourselves, our bodies, our womanhood when we've been taught that the divine is masculine. As we changed the "hims" to "hers" we woke up to an empowering and liberating experience. And at the same time got in touch with enormous grief and sorrow of living our lives so frequently invisible, even annihilated, disrespected and denied. In saying "she" instead of "he" also awakened us to the possibility of the wonder and joy of being valued, acknowledged, seen and admired—feeling our wholeness and sufficiency. It was very powerful and profound—a communal healing.

My response was intense. I started wailing. I tapped into, what felt like, a universal well of grief that was beyond myself. It is hard to put into words but I remember rocking back and forth sobbing uncontrollably. I connected to an ancient abyss of our collective grief that is part of our cultures, our global history, our female heritage. I felt an opening and receptivity to the possibility of reclaiming a humanity rooted in Earth Mother and a restoration of the divine, deep feminine (Feinstein, 2019).

Reception and Reactions

There seems to be an agreement among those I interviewed that the experiments organized by the Women's Caucus were instrumental in shifting the atmosphere at the institute toward one which was more inclusive and more welcoming. However, while the Women's Caucus was active, the institute was also undergoing its democratizing changes and the question comes to mind how these two important movements complemented each other. Both in their own way paid attention to what can be called the relational aspects of contacting. The women's perspective was influenced by feminism and the democratization of the institute drew inspiration from a new focus on group dynamics. Bloom comments on this development:

BLOOM: [The attention to the relational] came from a sense that by all that aggression of people arguing we weren't paying attention to the other side of it, how people were feeling about that kind of conversation. It came from the small groups and people being disgruntled there. And it came from women!

You speak to some of the women and they will talk about the feminist revolution. You know, it was the women who made the shift. And if you get to talk to Lee Zevy she will make a big point about that. I don't see it as that. I think that's kind of trivializing it. I think it was led by some women and I think it was an attention to people who were left out and women were leading that. But I think that was only the beginning of it. It was also some women. And men! And men who were saying that there was not something right about the fact that people were feeling left out (Bloom, 2019).

Bloom stresses the aspect of feeling left out and in this regard it may be impossible to discern the different effects the two movements had. But the women's cause was more than just about being left out. As I have already mentioned, feminism pursues a more fundamental goal which goes beyond "being included"; the aim is to uproot an age-old system of power imbalance based on gender. In this respect, there are indeed discernible effects that can be clearly attributed to the women's efforts. One of them is well captured by the following announcement of the institute's upcoming events from April 1992 (Klepner, 2020, 25):

Wednesday, May 13, 9 PM — MEN'S CAUCUS MEETING

Some concern has been expressed that a "feminization of the institute" is taking place. There has been lament by some for the "old days" of "rough and tumble" and high anxiety. But what is "masculine" style — Rough and Tumble? Competitive? Verbal? Dominating? — and what does this mean in terms of our theory? Can a field of human interaction be "masculinized" or "feminized"? Is the "split" in the field? In the genitals? In our projection of the introjections? The men of the institute are invited to meet to weigh these heavy issues and perhaps to define their own space(s) and articulate their own style(s).

Contact heals the splits, re-integrates the whole and, through the assimilation of the novel, creates the growth for new ways of relating in the environment and for new experiments. Perhaps in the Fall. AT: Richard Kitzler's Office, 140 West 16 Street, 2 East

If the democratization undid the fixed and no longer functional gestalt of the Fellows, then the women at the institute addressed a more fundamental fixity—that of patriarchal culture. Fixed gestalts are said to be part of the stabilizing structure. When they start to break down, feelings of loss, insecurity, and anxiety may arise. Some men—including Richard Kitzler, one of the main culprits of the combativeness that went on at the meetings—seemed so unsettled by the developments prompted by women that they felt a need for creating the Men's Caucus. Is it not a sign of men's position getting less secure? They sensed a loss ("lament for the old days") and they were forced to react. The creation of the Men's Caucus is thus a testimony to the success of the feminist efforts.

Let us now jump in time and look at the present situation. The change of the culture at the meetings brought about by the democratization of the institute and the Women's Caucus meant that some of the heated exchanges are no longer possible.

PHILIPPSON: In some way, this has been a real opening of the institute and people have felt more able to take part. In some way, there were elements of reaction formation so that it is difficult now to have an intense theoretical discussion. Some of the theoretical edge that I valued, while being put off sometimes by the style of it, is gone.

Dan Bloom describes this change in gestalt terms of figure/ground and identifies a new fixed gestalt. The conflicts at the meetings prior to 1990 were, according to Bloom, a *false figure* in the sense that it prevented other figures to emerge and left people feeling intimidated. There was nobody who would interrupt it and point to what is happening in the larger field of the group. Nowadays, Bloom continues, the situation flipped to its reverse, where there is not a support for a figure of conflict to emerge:

BLOOM: Let me give you an example: At a meeting, a figure of disagreement will emerge. And as soon as a sharp figure like this emerges it's stopped and somebody says: "Wait a minute. It feels like you're attacking" (Bloom, 2019).

In Bloom's view, the conflict is interrupted but an exploration of its ground does not take place, questions such as *What was it like for you?* are not asked and the interpretation that it was an attack is accepted as a given. Aggression is labeled as hostility and suppressed in consequence, argues Bloom. Instead of supporting initiative for coming forward, there is a support for what he calls "leveling," that is, not allowing the sharp figure of conflict to emerge.

BLOOM: For example, we have a meeting where somebody is talking. [Then someone interjects:] "Hold on a minute, I'd like to hear from somebody who hasn't talked, who hasn't spoken." That is a very common cliché that happens. Well, in my experience, sometimes somebody hasn't spoken because that person does not want to speak and does not want to be paid attention to. And that isn't honored. And that sometimes gets in the way.

For Bloom, the way the group process is currently handled at the institute represents a new fixed gestalt:

BLOOM: As much as I like the idea of making sure we pay attention that everybody in the room has a chance to speak, to stop an active discussion—which is a spontaneous, emerging figure, which has excitement, clarity and vitality, which is also involving people as their interest is pulled into it—to stop it, because this person there may not be involved and to try to get everybody involved is a fixed gestalt and does a violence to the entire whole. That I have seen happened more than once. That I'm against. And that's an example of taking an important good that was necessary and turning it into one more style of oppression.

I've seen it happen too many times; the consequence is that I pull back. And I know personally that my own style of active, excited engagement with another person has been misinterpreted as excluding others.

Bloom also raises the point that these developments need to be understood in the current context of the training structure at the institute. The small training groups, where the bonding used to happen and which were a source of support for coming forward at the large meetings, do not currently exist. Without them, the affiliation at the large meetings is made more difficult. Gregory corroborates Bloom's account:

GREGORY: It is different now from the old days when the meetings were large numbers of people, each belonging to study groups and the study groups would come together to the meeting. The next week, when the study group met again, they would discuss what went on in the meeting. So the studying and the meetings were integrated. This does not happen now.

Bloom concludes that the institute is still searching for a group process that could balance different styles of engagement. Those who had felt put off by the old style of the meetings have been given more room but in turn those who had not felt put off are now "crowded out," according to Bloom.

One way to look at this new conflict at the institute is through the prism of ethics and morality. As I have mentioned in Chapter 1, the original standpoint of gestalt therapy can be characterized as immoral ethics. It emphasizes organismic self-regulation and authenticity and looks suspiciously at morality which is seen to a large degree as self-conquest or resentment. Contrary to that, the process in which a strong figure of argument or conflict is disengaged because it is labeled as hostility or attacking, or because it may exclude others, seems to bring in the aspect of morality. Some of the elements and trends in various movements around social justice and responsibility directly and intentionally appeal to our conscience and enforce certain styles or norms of group interactions. This may be an efficient political strategy in the struggle to achieve important goals of equality and justice but from the perspective of gestalt therapy theory such fixed norms can also be seen as inhibiting introjects: certain vital parts of the creative and spontaneous individual and group self are suppressed. This makes for an uncomfortable mix. The "foreign body" of morality cannot be easily incorporated into the theory without compromising some of its foundational concepts such as introjection and organismic self-regulation. It puts the institute into a new predicament where the usual self-reflective application of gestalt therapy theory arrives at its limits. Although, in my view, the Women's Caucus already found a viable answer to this problem: the women used the feminist theories (also a foreign element in a sense) to understand something of importance about the dynamics at the institute, but they also managed to translate this knowledge into experiments which engaged the whole community. Their insight could actually be *experienced* by the members and so it shifted the communal awareness instead of only enforcing certain norms. In other words, through the process of awareness raising the community was in a position to assimilate the novelty.

Individualism vs. Feminism

Not all women from the institute were part of the caucus from the beginning. Susan Gregory recalls that she was not invited when it started but joined it once the caucus called on all the institute's women to join. Gregory offers a perspective of a woman who was not intimidated by the male-dominated style at the meetings:

GREGORY: I think the Women's Caucus was super important to the women here. They had allowed themselves to be members of this institute as secondary members, where they were afraid. I was never afraid, I didn't even get what they were saying! But that's the truth, they were all afraid—of the guys with the loud voices and the authoritarian behaviors, and the fighting and the argument. They didn't find that a female way to talk which is to speak and listen, then speak again and then listen. None of that was going on. It was the guys shouting and interrupting each other. They described that as male style and they wanted to do several different things to make functioning in the group as a woman easier and more seen (Gregory, 2019).

Gregory's view is reminiscent of Laura Perls's. Similarly to her, Gregory did not feel threatened or intimidated by the loud men at the meetings. On the contrary, she felt comfortable enough so that when women such as Zevy or Feinstein were framing the issue as a conflict between male and female ways of being, Gregory had her difficulty at first to understand their discontent. Her formulation "they allowed themselves to be [...] secondary members" comes from a perspective where the focus is on contact interruptions between individuals rather than—which would be the feminist view—on the *conditions* of contact-making. The difference between the two perspectives was well captured by Friedman (2000) in the presentation which she gave at the New York Institute. She compared her experiences from a gestalt group therapy and a feminist consciousness-raising group and she made the following distinction: whereas in her gestalt group the emphasis was on finishing an unfinished business (e.g., voicing a held back resentment), the feminist group focused on staying with the unfinished business and exploring the field in which it occurs. Friedman gives an example of a result of the latter approach:

> Let's take the topic of 'Competence' as an example. One of our discoveries was that we suffered from what we came to call programmed incompetence. One woman told us it was her role to read the map while her husband did the driving. As he drove he could demand of her that she find where they were, help him understand the route, read the road signs, coordinate the passages to connecting routes, fumble with the enormous folds of paper spread out before her face, absorb the pressures of his need to know on the spot, and absorb his annoyance with her if she needed time to understand it herself. Upon arrival at their destination, he, the driver, had earned the credit for his mastery. If they were lost or delayed, she would absorb the blame by way of humorous remarks about her inability to handle the map-reading efficiently. [...] We came to know in consciousness-raising that we, as women knew [...] how to read the map. We knew what went into reading the map. We knew the way we were related to as we read the map, and we knew we would end up in an unempowered position no matter what our input.

Friedman's account shows how women's experiences are validated and illuminated in the feminist approach. In a situation which is set up such that one cannot possibly respond with a satisfying action, ending up with the so-called unfinished business seems to be an obvious inevitability. In gestalt therapy terminology, the feminist approach can be characterized as field-oriented. To achieve its goal of empowerment and emancipation, it uses a combination of (a) description of personal experience, (b) social and political analysis, and (c) action in the community. The difficulty one experiences in a given situation is understood less as a personal failing or unused potential and more as a source of information about the environment. That is what Friedman meant by staying with the unfinished business.

Regarding the pair of description and action, one could say that here the feminist approach overlaps with gestalt therapy's phenomenological and experimental orientation. When it comes to analysis, it seems to me, that it is where these two approaches differ from each other in a significant way. From the perspective of feminism, which for obvious reasons relies on a particular analysis of social and political structures, gestalt therapy lacks an elaborated social theory. Indeed, in *Gestalt Therapy*, the social criticism rarely goes further than to point out how social institutions intervene negatively with the organismic self-regulation of an individual; moreover, this individual appears as genderless,[2] classless, raceless, etc. To the extent that gestalt therapy theory is understood in a field-oriented way, the exploration of the field conditions is part of the therapeutic process, but there are no particular theoretical lenses prescribed with which to do so.

It is an instinct of an overly individualistic culture to blame the individual for any perceived deficiency. The argument goes along the line "only if she stopped blocking herself and stopped being so manipulative she could find a way how to deal with her problems." In this imbalanced view, the sociopolitical conditions are disregarded and all becomes purely personal: from the experienced difficulty to the solution of the problem. A therapy which is not critical of its own ideological rootedness in individualism can instill a feeling of insufficiency and shame in the client. Friedman recalls her own experience from her gestalt group:

> When asked to tell my parents what I resented, I had no voice. This revelation to myself and the group generated a terrible feeling of shame in me. The shame came from the feeling that I was not even able to perform the therapeutic experiment.
>
> (Friedman, 2000, 2)

It is simply a poor therapy if one tries to undo an alleged block without considering the wider context in which it appears. Conversely, when the context is sufficiently explored, then the experienced difficulty often loses its character of a personal failure and is understood as a creative adjustment to the communal or political aspects, or better still, as a kind of knowledge of the situation. In her philosophical novel *Aliens and Anorexia*, Chris Kraus (2003) makes this latter point clearly. Kraus shows how in the history of psychiatry and philosophy, female emotionality was often interpreted and devalued as a manipulative behavior, a means to achieve a personal goal indirectly (e.g. anorexia as attention-seeking). But what if emotional suffering—in any of its form including depression, panic attacks, or anorexia—was seen as a form of knowledge and a direct answer to the situation? In this view, the female discontent can and should be interpreted as *impersonal* thus shedding light on society. The women of the Women's Caucus did exactly this kind of field exploration. They took their own feelings of discouragement and let it inform them about the structure of the field in which it manifested; and the tools they used to describe and dismantle the fixities of the community at the institute were the feminist theories and experimentation in the best sense of gestalt therapy. By doing so, they avoided the argumentative dead end of a naive form of individualism which would oblige them to address their own "personal" difficulties first. This does not mean that they avoided facing their fears. Remember Greenberg's words: the experiments themselves felt radical and daring. In a way they transformed the difficulty, the anxiety, the fear, etc. from personal into communal and further still into socio-political.

The gestalt therapy theory, as presented by the joint work of Perls and Goodman, is an integration of both approaches, the one that focuses on the individual's growth, independence, self-reliance, self-regulation, etc., and the one which considers the living conditions in the socio-political context. Toward the end of the theory part of *Gestalt Therapy*, we can find a short passage demonstrating how these two approaches represent two aspects of the same process:

> The psychotherapy we propose emphasizes: concentrating on the struc-
> ture of the actual situation; preserving the integrity of the actuality by
> finding the intrinsic relation of sociocultural, animal, and physical fac-
> tors; experimenting; promoting creative power of the patient to reinte-
> grate dissociated parts.
>
> (Perls et al., 1994, 13)

The language of creativity and dissociated parts expresses the polarity of the individual whereas concentrating on the structure of the actual situation with its intrinsic socio-cultural aspects considers the wider context. We can see that theory of gestalt therapy, when properly understood, integrates these two polarities in its unitary approach.

> The human organism/environment is, of course, not only physical but
> social. So in any humane study, such as human physiology, psychol-
> ogy, or psychotherapy, we must speak of a field in which at least social-
> cultural, animal, and physical factors interact. Our approach in this
> book is "unitary" in the sense that we try in a detailed way to consider
> every problem as occurring in a social-animal-physical field. From this
> point of view, for instance, historical and cultural factors cannot be con-
> sidered as complicating or modifying conditions of a simpler biophysical
> situation, but are intrinsic in the way any problem is presented to us.
>
> (Perls et al., 1994, 4–5)

The history of the New York Institute illustrates how the gestalt approach (inseparably individualistic *and* field-oriented) coincides in an interesting way with activism. The creation of Identity House and the unmasking of homophobia as a societal pathology (Chapter 2), the democratization of the institute with its accompanying shift of focus from the hot-seat work toward group dynamics (Chapter 3), and, finally, the institute's feminist revolution described in this chapter are all examples of this gestalt/activist approach.

Notes

1 Personal correspondence.
2 Though of course referred to as he. That is the irony.

Bibliography

Bloom, D. (2019). Interviewed on March 6, 2019.

Feinstein, G. (2019). Interviewed on April 24, 2019.

Firestone, S. (1972). *The dialectic of sex: The case for feminist revolution.* Bantam Books.

Friedman, Z. (2000). *The gestalt of feminism.* A draft of NYIGT presentation. Not published.

Greenberg, E. (2019). Interviewed on March 6, 2019.

Gregory, S. (2019). Interviewed on March 14, 2019.

Klepner, P. (2020). Collection of the NYIGT's meeting reports and letters to membership. Not published.

Kraus, C. (2003). *Aliens & Anorexia.* Semiotext(e).

Perls, F., Hefferline, R. F., & Goodman, P. (1994). *Gestalt therapy: Excitement and growth in the human personality.* The Gestalt Journal Press, Inc.

Rosenblatt, D. (1994). Laura Perls – further memories and reflections. *The British Gestalt Journal,* 3(1), 22–31.

Zevy, L. (2019). Interviewed on April 5, 2019.

Chapter 5

Internationality

The New York Institute was for a longer period of time a rather insular organization which did not keep close contacts with other gestalt institutes. As Zevy (2019) put it: "There was a side of the institute that was arrogant to the point of believing they had the keys to kingdom and everybody needed to follow theoretically along a certain line or you were lesser than." This started to change approximately in the second half of the 1970s when the members of the second or third generation—those who were students of Laura Perls, Richard Kitzler, Isadore From, Karen Humphrey, Patrick Kelley, etc.—were coming into their own. They did not have to defend gestalt therapy against psychoanalysis and the polarization between the West and East Coast styles was also weakening. They were more open to new influences and started to collaborate with other institutes. An example of such collaborations is the book *Beyond the Hot Seat*, which was published in 1980 and was edited by Bud Feder and Ruth Ronall (both New York Institute members). It was a collection of papers from 16 authors, of which ten were from other institutes. The reputation of the institute at that time was not flattering—according to Greenberg, people from other local institutes looked at the New York group as being "snooty, mean, rejecting, and fighting all the time" (Greenberg, 2019)—and so this new generation of members had the additional task of overcoming this reputation.

In the 1990s, the landscape of gestalt therapy in the USA and Europe was already broad and varied and the interest of the wider gestalt community to meet and collaborate was also growing. In 1992, the Association for the Advancement of Gestalt Therapy[1] (AAGT) was established. A number of people from the New York Institute were helping to shape the AAGT from the start—Bud Feder, for example, or Carl Hodges, who was the AAGT President from 1995 to 1997. Simultaneously, the younger members of the New York Institute started to write and publish on gestalt theory and practice. The generation of the Fellows was not very active in this respect. Laura Perls, Richard Kitzler, Isadore From, Karen Humphrey, and Patrick Kelley were considered brilliant therapists and teachers; their written output however was relatively meager. According to Zevy (2019), their resistance

DOI: 10.4324/9781003296539-6

to writing "became almost embodied into theoretical perspective that the greatest sin was the bureaucratization of the prophetic, so everything was organized around never letting that happen." At the time they were trying to align theory and practice along gestalt therapy principles, a noble effort, but as time went on, this became too narrow an interpretation. In the 1980s, Richard Kitzler's study group moved away from the book *Gestalt Therapy* and began to study theory and philosophy starting with Aristotle, then moving to writers like James and Mead, and then to return to *Gestalt Therapy* and examine the founding text from new perspectives.

The younger generation was interested in developing the theory and they were writing, and publishing, and they started getting invited to teach and work with gestalt therapists abroad. Zevy (2019) continues:

ZEVY: Isadore's, Fritz's, and Laura's teaching was having a profound effect on Europe. When the Italians picked it up in the 1990s and Margherita [Spagnuolo Lobb] became involved she invited members of the institute to visit and to work with the people in Sicily. The New York Institute started to develop a process-oriented model. When we went to Sicily it was to teach the New York Institute way of perspective of seeing. Joe [Lay] was there, Karen [Humphrey] was there, I was there, Carl [Hodges] came. Through Dan Bloom's initiative this led to the NYIGT opening up itself to non-local members and the institute expanded widely.

For Margherita Spagnuolo Lobb, the connection to the New York Institute began in 1980 in California. She took part in training by Erving and Miriam Polsters in La Jolla where she met Isadore From whom Polsters invited regularly as a guest-trainer. She was impressed by From's therapeutic skill and started to train with him and invite him to teach at her institute in Italy. He introduced the Italian group to the founding text—*Gestalt Therapy* by Perls, Hefferline, and Goodman—and to the people at the New York Institute. Spagnuolo Lobb remembers:

SPAGNUOLO LOBB: First I met the book and then I met the people. And I liked them! I felt at home very soon at the institute. They were theoretical but not exclusively, they also liked to dance and move. I experienced these people as very alive (Spagnuolo Lobb, 2021).

After Isadore From's death in 1994, the contact between Spagnuolo Lobb and the New Yorkers intensified. Richard Kitzler, who lost his theoretical arch enemy[2] and anyway mellowed over time, was now the main figure at the institute. He supported Spagnuolo Lobb's efforts for cooperation between her institute in Syracuse, Sicily and the NYIGT. He also eventually proposed her name for full membership. In 1997, the Istituto di Gestalt and the NYIGT organized a joint conference under the name TransAtlantic

Dialogs. This conference took place in New York. A year later, as President of the European Association for Gestalt Therapy (EAGT), Spagnuolo Lobb oversaw a conference in Palermo to which she also invited her colleagues from New York.

SPAGNUOLO LOBB: The conference was huge! There were I think 400 people, very much a novelty at that time. In the general meeting I proposed to nominate the New York Institute as the honorary member of the EAGT because it was the founding institute of gestalt therapy. They rejected this proposal. I was the President but they rejected it. They did not recognize the New York Institute as the place where gestalt therapy was founded. [...] Many thought gestalt therapy was created by Perls in Esalen. This was painful on one hand but we also looked at ourselves in the mirror. We recognized our reality (Spagnuolo Lobb, 2021).

The tensions and polarizations between the West and East Coast were still palpable at that time. When Claudio Naranjo, who had trained with Fritz Perls in California, and Dan Bloom, who was then President of the New York Institute, met at a conference in Naples in 2002, they still had old wounds that needed to be addressed. They shared a stage and were fighting. Naranjo was scolding Dan Bloom and the New York Institute that they did not honor the founder, Fritz Perls, enough. After 40 years since Fritz's funeral, the harsh eulogy that Paul Goodman gave at that occasion still pained Naranjo's memory. And he might not have been completely off the mark with his critique either: in Philippson's view, the New Yorkers were influenced by Laura Perls who "was very angry with Fritz and presented herself as the good guy and Fritz as the bad guy" (Philippson, 2021). As if the marital troubles of Laura and Fritz sent powerful ripples through the field of gestalt therapy and decades later they were still echoing and shaping the field.

Another interesting event that happened around that time was the so-called *Miracle of Lipari*. In 2001, about 20 people from Spagnuolo Lobb's institute and 14 people from the New York Institute met in on the Aeolian island Lipari for a week-long retreat:

SPAGNUOLO LOBB: It was an experiment with no topic. We were together on this small island in an old, no longer used church. We had no rules. Not all of us spoke English. So there were people who could not understand each other. We just stayed together to see what happens. [...] We went through curiosity, sometimes boredom, and then anger, because we could not understand each other, and then fear and craziness and then more, better curiosity and trust and spontaneity. And in the final round we were all standing in a circle. The feeling was that every one of us could do or say whatever he or she wanted to in that moment and in that situation and everybody else would have listened. So we had the feeling that we could come forward and could say anything and we would be understood even if in another language. [...] As if a talented director had organized all this but nobody had organized it, it was self-regulated. [...] At the end there was a big applause and we all felt very close to each other. Richard many times asked me to write something about this Miracle of Lipari [that is how Richard Kitzler described the event] but I never had the time unfortunately.

There were also other conferences and occasions where the two institutes met but my intention here is not to provide an exhaustive account of these events. Rather, I would like to convey the sense of the opening of the NY-IGT toward the international members and, vice versa, to show how this group became more internationally recognized and relevant. Another person from abroad who became a full member early on was Peter Philippson:

PHILIPPSON: I attended conferences in the United States of the Gestalt Journal. I went to the conference in Chicago in 1989 and Manhattan Beach and Los Angeles in 1991. I met a lot of the New York people then. I got a sense of them as holding something from the beginnings of gestalt therapy which was outside of what I've been taught. Another part of that was that a part of my background, and that of John Harris with whom I was working, was a group work. We were group workers before we were gestalt therapists. And yet what we've been taught in terms of gestalt therapy kept the group work and the gestalt therapy very separate. At some stage in the 1980s, we read Bud Feder's and Ruth Ronall's edited book Beyond the Hot Seat and got very excited. Because this was a support for us bringing together two worlds. And they became kind of gurus for us at that time. And it was lovely going to the conferences and meeting Bud and Ruth and getting on with them very well (Philippson, 2021).

Philippson invited Bud Feder to come to train at Manchester Gestalt Center. During his visit, Feder was staying at Philippson's and the two befriended each other. "This guru of mine ended up teaching my kids Indian leg wrestling," reminisces Philippson (2021) fondly. In the early 1990s, Philippson started going to the New York Institute's meetings; he would stay at Feder's place in New Jersey or with Susan Gregory in proximity of Brooklyn Bridge.

PHILIPPSON: I remember going on the bus from Montclair, New Jersey into the Port Authority, New York and it was like magic! It went down into the Lincoln Tunnel and before that it was kind of open countryside and then it came up in the middle of Manhattan. It was like the whole scene had changed! (Philippson, 2021)

Philippson's amazement at the change of the scenery continued at the meetings:

PHILIPPSON: I found [the institute meetings] quite an amazing thing. There was a real culture of linking theory and practice, arguing with each other in a very New York sort of way, which took a bit of time to acclimatize to it. But it wasn't completely unfamiliar for me because in my jewish family similar things happened (Philippson, 2021).

According to Philippson, the New York Institute fulfills two main functions: first, it is the early home of gestalt therapy and as such it holds the history and second, it is a home-base for its community.

PHILIPPSON: My initial intention in joining was to have support for the way I was getting to understand gestalt therapy. So it was in that function of being a sort of founding institute. But inevitably it also became a kind of home institute for me and I took my kids across. Me, Bud and my kids went rowing on the Delaware river, I went round the art galleries with Susan Gregory, stayed at times with Lee and Burt and my wife and me went to Dan's wedding. So, in a way I guess I was the sort of acceptable end of that dichotomy. Because I had enough time and space to do both sides of that. Whereas people who came later would have less personal involvement (Philippson, 2021).

In 1995, there was a discussion around this topic and the decision was made that the institute was going to accept international members. However, this opening in the second function created new tensions at the institute. The community became gradually more dispersed and some of the newcomers did not have the close personal connections with the rest of the community. For some members it meant a painful loss of the feeling of a home and family. In 2015, Bud Feder recalled:

One of the reasons I'm not very active any more is because other people, not me, decided they wanted to make the New York Institute an international institute. They have brought in members from other countries like France and Italy. To me, it has changed the flavor. The New York Institute, particularly during my years of struggle, was my second family. [...] It has lost, to me, my personal connection and the current institute no longer has the place in my heart that the original institute did.

(Feder, 2015)

But there are also counterexamples: For Ruella Frank the presence of people from Italy and France meant that she could find a way how to reconnect with the institute which after the death of Richard Kitzler and departure of other friends left her with a sense of missing. She attends the meetings sporadically now but she feels communal with the members from Europe: "when Jean-Marie comes, or Margherita comes, I'm always there"[3] (Frank 2019). And from Spagnuolo Lobb's (2021) angle:

SPAGNUOLO LOBB: It felt normal to me to approach the New York Institute as my home. I always considered the institute as a point of reference. It's the place where gestalt therapy was born. For me it's natural that the international people address the New York Institute as a point of reference. I teach my students that gestalt therapy was founded there. So they see the institute like an icon. [...] I think it is natural that the New York Institute has to open itself to the international people but I also understand that for those who are local members, they might find themselves lost without a local identity.

Additionally, the fact that increasingly more members were not living in New York brought up the question of the value of in-person vs. online meetings. Especially during Adam Weitz' Presidency this question was grappled with and interestingly, it was the younger people who were asking for more face-to-face (Zevy, 2019). In 2020, the COVID-19 pandemic changed the field completely: group meetings were suddenly not possible and video conferencing became a normality. In 2020, many more members from abroad joined the institute and in comparison to the previous year, the membership numbers seem to have doubled.[4]

ZEVY: More and more people from other countries are interested in joining the institute because we have the history as the original institute. How to work that is the big question now, right? I want to spread out the administration since we can have people work online. Let's get a president who lives in another country! It does not matter at this point. Great resistance to that! "No! we are the New York Institute, face-to-face is important!" (Zevy, 2019)

Zevy's suggestion that the next President could be a person from abroad did not gain a support first, but the recent developments in connection with the pandemic may eventually tilt the leaning. Since what is the meaning of a local President in an organization that is increasingly international? The current proposal, which tries to address this conundrum of local and non-local members is to organize two meetings per month, one online and one in-person. Only time and experience will show what this new experiment will bring, whether it will sharpen the shape of the community or create some kind of a split.

Another question which interested me in my interviews with Spagnuolo Lobb and Philippson was whether their own respective local institutes adopted some of the form of functioning and organizing of the New York Institute.

SPAGNUOLO LOBB: It was very influential! Because Isadore told us the history of the institute. He recounted how they met and the spirit of their meeting. And we started to create this function of teaching/learning community at our institute. We were together and we worked on ourselves as a group and we also had theoretical discussions. Theoretical discussions and working on some group process was the same thing (Spagnuolo Lobb, 2021).

PHILIPPSON: I think it's more like that there are kind of parallels by which we recognize each other. Manchester gestalt Centre was going since 1988 and we've never had a director. We had been working as a collective throughout. We are running a certified gestalt training, but there is a push towards people who are in adult education and who come in with their own expertise. We want them to bring in their own thinking and so we are really encouraging difference. We also invite trainers who have very different ideas so that people get experiences outside of what the Manchester trainers do and how they put it. So that's quite similar while at the same time it's different in that we actually run a training program leading to accreditation (Philippson, 2021).

The fact that the NYIGT does not provide certification allows the institute to maintain a certain radicalness in the way it organizes itself. It can maintain an independence from bureaucratic requirements, avoid a fixed hierarchical structure, and attract people for different reasons than obtaining an official certificate. Therefore, even if other institutes are inspired by some of the NYIGT's functioning—such as the concept of teaching/learning community; contact and experimentation as the spring board of new organizational structures; or the readiness to identify and destroy dysfunctional gestalts—they are limited in incorporating radically these principles by the fact that they have to provide specific curricula and that the students who train there pursue the concrete goal of graduation for which they usually pay a significant amount of money. The New York Institute still maintains its unique identity but because of its increasing internationalization and the shift from in-person meetings to the online format, it starts to take on the shape of an association rather than an institute. It is a question whether it will be able to maintain a recognizable identity next to other gestalt associations, especially in comparison to the International Association for the Advancement of Gestalt Therapy which is built on very similar organizing principles.

Notes

1 In 2020, the association renamed itself to "International Association for the Advancement of Gestalt Therapy".
2 Recall how From and Kitzler were leading their proxy wars at the institute meetings, each attacking the presenters from the opponent's training groups (Chapter 1).
3 Jean-Marie Robine and Margherita Spagnuolo Lobb.
4 This is just a rough estimate based on the list of members available at the institute's homepage.

Bibliography

Feder, B. (2015). *Origins of gestalt therapy.* Retrieved from https://youtu.be/NZSEuN7QrTs
Frank, R. (2019). Interviewed on March 7, 2019.
Greenberg, E. (2019). Interviewed on March 6, 2019.
Philippson, P. (2021). Interviewed on June 15, 2021.
Spagnuolo Lobb, M. (2021). Interviewed on May 26, 2021.
Zevy, L. (2019). Interviewed on April 5, 2019.

Conclusion

Recall the crisis at the end of the 1980s: every Fellow at that point has been the Vice President or the Treasurer or the Secretary and none of them had the appetite for a second service. They were worn out (Feder, 2015) and were not rejuvenating (Klepner, 2019). They therefore turned to the Full Members and sought the new officers there. That was a moment when the new generation took over and radically reshaped the institute. It seems that the institute is currently at a similar turning point where there is a transfer between generations and the future form of the institute is unclear and in making. Adam Weitz, the President of the institute from 2017 to 2019, described this situation in gestalt terms as the fertile void and gave the following account:

> WEITZ: The older people who have put hours and hours of love and labor into this Institute from the get-go—most of whom had studied with Laura and so they still have that touch to the rock of Medina—are kind of done. Not done with their care for the institute, not done with their affection for gestalt therapy, not done with their amity and love for each other. They are not done with that. But they're done with stuffing envelopes. They have worked! Most of them didn't miss a meeting for twenty five, or thirty or forty years. At all! Ever! (Weitz, 2019).

The turning point, according to Weitz, is that, on the one hand, the older generation is worn out—some of them served multiple times as Vice Presidents and Bloom and Zevy served two presidential terms—but, on the other hand, they are reluctant to transfer the reins to the newer generation. Asked why she served as the President for a second time, Zevy replied that the institute "did not have enough new people to step in who were sufficiently familiar with the theory and practice of gestalt therapy and the workings of the institute" (Zevy, 2019). At the same time, the younger generation is not enthusiastic about taking over: at the beginning of 2019, Weitz put out two calls for officers for the institute's executive committee but no one came forward. For a while it looked like there would not be a person willing to serve

DOI: 10.4324/9781003296539-7

as the next President. In a development which parallels the situation at the institute at the end of the 1980s, the younger generation refuses to take over the institute in the shape it was handed to them. Also then, in 1991 Karen Humphrey expressed her concern about the readiness of the institute's upcoming generation:

> What I am concerned about is that as we lose our senior people, I'm not sure that we have another generation that is really up to it, that can attract people to them the way certainly Laura and Isadore [did].
>
> (Robine, 1991)

Reflecting on the situation in 2019, Adam Weitz comments that there has not been a sufficient transfer of the essence of the institute's unique, hard-to-grasp, and fluid functioning. The needs and expectations regarding the institute changed and the younger members are asking for a different type of functioning which seems to be at cross-purposes with the foundational Goodmanian conception of an organismically self-regulating teaching-learning community. For example, according to Weitz, the new generation wants more structure and support than the original idea of self-supporting membership and non-bureaucratic functioning envisioned. I have asked Weitz whether he could find his own formulation of what the essence of the New York Institute is. He gave this answer:

WEITZ: These words are going to sound to anyone who is not a gestalt therapist totally ridiculous: attending to what is; continuously attending to what is and naming it; our shape is an ongoing process; paying attention and engaging with one another around that ongoing process; setting up our programs and deciding what we are going to do together emerge out of our own processing of what is for us and for the institute as a field phenomenon; not being attached to any one shape, except the shape of ongoing change; continuing to understand ourselves as a gestalt therapy experiment and finding language to describe ourselves out of gestalt therapy language and concepts; evolve those concepts if necessary, if that is emergent for us all; to be as contactful as possible with each other as individuals, as people; and also to turn our attention to what Carl Hodges would have called the self of group; there is a self of our organization which is itself contacting the world and a field phenomenon—which includes ourselves; this ongoing way of looking at being a community is the essence; not rushing to premature resolution of conflict, of anything; staying with what is and experimenting; understanding each season as an experiment, each program year as an experiment, each endeavor as an experiment. This is how I see it. It is an Aristotelian shape—a process oriented shape (Weitz, 2019).

The shape of the institute seems to be currently in the making again. A new figure emerges and it is anybody's guess what it will be. If this new figure should follow the principle of organismic self-regulation, as envisioned by Perls and Goodman, then it will grow out of the concrete needs of the community. These needs still have to be made aware, named, and finally allowed to spontaneously contact the actuality. My impression is that the growing international membership, especially those who joined relatively recently, observe the community with curiosity but also from a distance. Somewhat like in the fishbowl experiments. Those in the smaller circle—the core of the institute—are doing the interesting work and those in the larger circle are trying to figure out the inner workings of the community; they are not yet fully involved and they may still not feel that they are responsible for the future shape of the institute. But they are. The furnace where the shape is forged is the process of contacting and creative conflict and everyone has a say in it. But there are also differences between the inner and the outer circle. The generation which trained with Laura Perls, Richard Kitzler, Isadore From, Karen Humphrey, and Patrick Kelley all have the experience of the smaller training groups where they got to know each other intimately and bore witness to the highs and lows of each other. Also, many of them share the experience of coming out and establishing their identity as members of the LGBT+ community which they supported through different forms of activism. Going through the trenches of relationships and personal development creates a lasting trust which becomes a part of the ground of contacting. There are some international members like Spagnuolo Lobb or Peter Philippson who also have a share in this bonding even though they were not part of the early training groups. But with them, too, personal relationships and going through "stuff" together played a crucial role. Philippson came regularly to New York and Spagnuolo Lobb invited the New York Institute for Gestalt Therapy (NY-IGT) members to Italy; they organized and participated in meetings, conferences, workshop, retreats. Over time they created close friendships. The outer circle does not have this extent of the shared experience; those members joined the institute out of fascination for its history, for its unique way of functioning, out of affection for their New York trainers and so on, but there is not the degree of bonding among them as there is in the group that attracted them. It remains to be seen whether they, too, will have the opportunity to connect intimately among each other or they will be more in a role of curious tourists. The dynamics of tourism has the potential to hollow up the substance of its destination. Will the community at the NYIGT follow this path in which it will end up performing that which the spectators expect to see or will it retain its liveliness and rejuvenate? Will the principles of gestalt therapy (and their goal of excitement and growth) keep sustaining it?

Bibliography

Feder, B. (2015). *Origins of gestalt therapy.* Retrieved from https://youtu.be/
NZSEuN7QrTs

Klepner, P. (2019). Interviewed on March 8, 2019.

Robine, J. -M. (1991). Interview with Karen Humphrey. Retrieved from https://
newyorkgestalt.org/1991-interview-with-karen/

Weitz, A. (2019). Interviewed on April 27, 2019.

Zevy, L. (2019). Interviewed on April 5, 2019.

Afterword

By Adam Weitz

Václav Mikolášek's well-researched book has caused me to reflect upon my own history of learning gestalt therapy theory and practice by absorbing it as a member of the New York Institute for Gestalt Therapy (NYIGT). I want to offer a few illustrations of my experience of "absorbing" gestalt therapy.

I am remembering sitting in a circle at a NY Institute meeting held in the Identity House meeting room. Alive in my body, I looked and listened, absorbing gestalt therapy in the process. I experienced the meaning of gestalt therapy theoretical terms, such as introject or field, in the context of the moment. Peter Philippson was presenting that day. After much hesitation, I spoke. I don't remember what I said, but I do remember Peter's response, which was, "Behind what you're saying is a need. What are you needing right now?" I remember feeling embarrassed and exposed. Yet, through this, I learned to consider what a person might be needing in the background to what they are saying or doing.

Mikolášek wrote at length about aggression in the style of the New York Institute. I remember a meeting presentation focused on conflict. We explored working-through conflict while remaining in contact with one another. I was able to chew on and ultimately reject an introject I had been carrying that "all conflict is bad." Interactions that may have been seen as aggressive by some, were fruitful conflicts from which I and the community grew. I vividly remember our aware community experience of aggression and conflict. As a result of that meeting, I carry with me a belief in the value of staying with and not prematurely resolving potentially growthful conflict.

Often, when I walked into Institute meetings, Karen Humphrey would give me a welcoming nod and a reassuring smile. Her smile helped me offset the intimidating quality of the room. Karen's smile is emblematic of a warmth and comradery, which to this day exists alongside the institute's well-known aggression.

I recall an instance when I described my experience of speaking up, sharing, "I feel as if I'm about to 'walk the plank' out into the center of this circle." Bud Feder, who was President at the time, said, "I thought we had left that behind." By that, Bud meant the intimidating, scary quality of speaking up at a NYIGT meeting. Though it was no doubt less scary than the "hammering" of earlier institute gatherings described by Elliot Shapiro, the institute hadn't left it behind. This was OK. Finding a way to speak up, finding my voice, risking it, has been an invaluable part of my experiential learning at NYIGT.

Just as described by the interviewees in Mikolášek's book, small group study experiences supported my learning in the whole group monthly meetings. I worked with Susan Gregory every week, and often processed the whole group meeting experience with her. I attended a wonderful study group with Carl Hodges and for a time was part of a peer group of NYIGT members. It was in this peer group that I first used the word "absorb" to describe my NYIGT study style.

New York Institute meetings have been infused with phenomenological awareness. I have come to understand gestalt therapy as an experience rather than an "aboutist" lesson. At their best, NYIGT meetings are not about gestalt therapy, NYIGT meetings are a process of gestalt therapy.

Writing these examples here has led me to think about what's possible for NYIGT's future. I would be curious to know what we might discover should Václav Mikolášek or another author undertake the same phenomenological interviewing process with those who are or were members in the 21st century. What could we learn about how the NYIGT functions right now and how it might function in the future? I look forward to reading such a text, expecting it to be as excellent as I found Mikolášek's to be.

Index

Note: Page numbers followed by "n" refer to end notes.

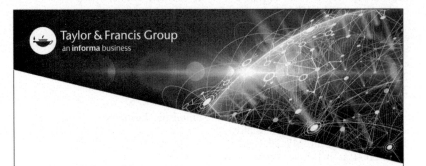